4981 8049

SO-BEZ-538

SPORTS DEVOTIONS
FOR ALL★STAR KIDS

Revised and Updated

DAVE BRANON

WITHDRAWN

BEAVERTON CITY LIBRARY
Beaverton, OR 97005
Member of Washington County
COOPERATIVE LIBRARY SERVICES

SPORTS DEVOTIONS
FOR ALL★STAR KIDS

DAVE BRANON

ZONDERkidz™
.com

We want to hear from you. Please send your comments about this book to us in care of zreview@zondervan.com. Thank you.

ZONDERKIDZ

Heads Up!
Copyright © 2012 by Dave Branon

This title is also available as a Zondervan ebook.
Visit www.zondervan.com/ebooks.

Requests for information should be addressed to:
Zonderkidz, *Grand Rapids, Michigan 49530*

Library of Congress Cataloging-in-Publication Data

Branon, Dave.
  Heads up! : sports devotions for all-star kids / Dave Branon. — [Updated ed.]
     p. cm.
  ISBN 978-0-310-72544-2 (softcover)
  1. Children—Prayers and devotions—Juvenile literature. 2. Sports—Religious aspects—
Christianity—Juvenile literature. I. Title.
  BV4870.B68 2012
  242'.62—dc23   2011036688

All Scripture quotations, unless otherwise indicated, are taken from the Holy Bible, *New International Version®*, *NIV®*. Copyright © 1973, 1978, 1984, 2011 by Biblica, Inc.™ Used by permission. All rights reserved worldwide.

Any Internet addresses (websites, blogs, etc.) and telephone numbers in this book are offered as a resource. They are not intended in any way to be or imply an endorsement by Zondervan, nor does Zondervan vouch for the content of these sites and numbers for the life of this book.

All rights reserved. No part of this publication may be reproduced, stored in a retrieval system, or transmitted in any form or by any means—electronic, mechanical, photocopy, recording, or any other—except for brief quotations in printed reviews, without the prior permission of the publisher.

Zonderkidz is a trademark of Zondervan.

Editor: Kim Childress
Cover design: Kris Nelson
Interior design: Ben Fetterly

Printed in the United States of America

---

12 13 14 15 16 17 18 19 20 21 22 23 24 25 26 /DCI/ 13 12 11 10 9 8 7 6 5 4 3 2 1

Foreword by Michelle Akers

Hey there! Welcome to *Heads Up!* I am so glad you're taking the time to check this book out, because it not only talks about sports and some very cool athletes, but it also brings to light the most important topic you'll ever consider in your lifetime: Jesus Christ.

Too often, it seems, we spend our lives chasing after fun times, popularity, lots of money, and other things, and we neglect the most important piece of who we are, what we're created for, and what will happen to us when we die.

Isn't it true? We spend so much time pursuing everything we think will make us cool or tough or popular, that when we finally find out that all this "stuff" isn't really important, we find ourselves confused, disheartened, and empty.

Soon we realize there has to be more to life than what we have spent all our time chasing. That's why this book (and other ones like it) is so important. It gives real-life answers to the big-time questions and shows us how much we mean to God.

Looking back, I can see that *Heads Up!* is exactly the kind of book I wish I'd had as a kid. It not only might have helped me steer clear of a lot of trouble and heartache, but it would also have helped me understand more about who God is, what he has in store for me if only I follow him, and the incredible privilege and gift of being his kid.

You see, when I became a Christian as a teenager, I didn't have much help spiritually. One desperate night, I turned my life over to Christ, and from then on, yes, I knew I was going to heaven—I even went to church and tried to study the Bible.

But since I didn't have much direction or guidance in how to continue growing up as a believer, it wasn't long before I began to lose focus.

As time passed, instead of growing stronger in my new-found faith, I began to fall back into my old habits. I eventually got carried away with my soccer and other activities that I thought would provide me with fun, friends, and personal value. It wasn't long before I had drifted from my relationship with Christ and God and got totally immersed in pursuing success and purpose on the soccer field.

It wasn't until my life had spun totally out of control and I had hit total rock bottom that I finally did what I should have done from the very beginning: I surrendered my heart, ambitions, and life to God.

Since that moment, life hasn't always been easy, but it has given me the answers, purpose, and adventure I was searching so desperately for from day one of my Christian life.

This book can help you avoid the trouble and heartache I got myself into over the years. It can help you understand that God has a unique and special plan for you, that he wants to have a relationship with you, and that there's nothing in the world more important or exciting than staying close to him and allowing him to work in and through you.

The other reason I like this book is because it's written by someone I know and trust. Dave Branon has been the editor of *Sports Spectrum* magazine for a long time, and over the years he has written several articles about me. He has also put me on the cover a few times, so you know he has got to be one of my faves! (Ha.)

No, really, in all seriousness, this is big-time stuff. Life-changing stuff. *Heads Up!* will guide you in not only how to get right with God but also how to grow strong in your faith and be a key player in God's ultimate plan for your future.

ROCK ON!
LOVE,
MICHELLE

Introduction

I needed somebody to give me a "heads up" a couple of times in my days as an athlete—but it didn't happen.

One time I took a baseball right in the nose because the ball came my way without anyone bothering to yell, "Heads up!" I was just eleven years old or so at the time, but I still remember how much it hurts to have a baseball rearrange your face.

Another time, I was playing college basketball when a player on the other team ran into me and split my chin open with his head. Again, I wish one of my buddies had warned me with a "Heads up!" before we collided.

It's good to get a heads-up call. Let's say you're at a baseball game, and you turn your head to holler at the hot-dog guy to bring you a couple of red hots. Suddenly, some Mark McGwire wannabe nails a high fastball and pulls it down the third baseline—right at your bean. As the ball locks in on your noggin, someone a few seats away screams, "Heads up!"

You know the drill. You duck and cover your head with your hands to protect your skull. The ball glances off your arm and bounces harmlessly to a guy about five rows away, who keeps it. At least he could offer you the ball, but hey, nobody's perfect.

In that kind of heads-up situation, you're grateful for those two words.

That's what I want this spiritual "Heads up!" to do for you. *Get Your Attention!*

Sometimes our attention gets turned away from God a little bit, and we need someone to wake us up before we get nailed with some problem we didn't see coming. That's one thing

Heads Up! can do for you—get you thinking about God in the middle of all the other stuff going on in your life.

There's another way to look at the term *heads up!* Sometimes you can get a little down about life. Things can get tough at home or at school. And even sports, which are supposed to be fun, can be a downer when you strike out or kick an own goal (a score on your own goal) or drive a tee shot into the water (if you're like me, you have those magical "water-seeking" golf-balls).

When those things happen, you need a friendly boost. Something to lift your head. To encourage you. To help you remember that you're pretty special.

It's my hope and prayer that this book will do those things for you. You'll read a lot of stories about Christian athletes and discover how they handle life. And you'll find out a whole bunch of information about making yourself a better athlete. But beyond all that, my main goal is for you to grow closer to God as you read.

That you'll keep your head up—and your eyes focused on Jesus Christ.

GAME PLAN

> Jesus answered, "I am the way and the truth and the life. No one comes to the Father except through me."
>
> John 14:6

Play Book Assignment: Read John 3:1–16

Which Way?

Did you ever shoot at the other team's basket during a basketball game? That's pretty embarrassing. But think of how embarrassing it would be to run a football all the way to the goal line—the wrong way! In the Rose Bowl!

Talk about going from glory to goat in five seconds flat!

It happened a long time ago. Before television. Maybe before radio. It was January 1, 1929, and the University of California was playing Georgia Tech in the huge Rose Bowl game in Pasadena, California. Roy Riegels of UC grabbed a Tech fumble and took off for all he was worth. After all, this was the biggest bowl game in college football, and he had a chance to make history. So he ran. And ran. And ran.

All the while, his teammates were running after him, trying to flag him down. Roy was running toward the wrong goal line. Finally, just before he would have carried the ball across for a Georgia Tech touchdown, one of his teammates tackled him. On the next play, California was sacked in the end zone for a safety, and they lost the game 8–7.

Ever since then, Roy Riegels has been known as Wrong Way Roy.

Did you ever think about whether you're going the right way? In life, that is. It happens to a lot of kids. Read this verse and think about what it means: "There is a way that seems right to a man, but in the end it leads to death" (Proverbs 14:12). In other words, people can think they're headed God's way only to discover that "Oops!" that wasn't it.

The right way to go is the way that Jesus says to go.

Here's what he said: "I am the way and the truth and the life. No one comes to the Father except through me" (John 14:6). That means that if you want to get to heaven, you need to put your faith in Jesus Christ.

Roy Riegels was so sincere. He was running his hardest. The closer he got to the goal line, the more convinced he was that he was headed in the right direction. He was doing his best and running his hardest. But he ran his team to a defeat.

Remember Wrong Way Roy and learn. Make sure you are going the right way. Jesus's way.

On the Chalkboard

The wrong way is always the long way.

Sports History Note

On January 1, 1902, the first Rose Bowl game was played. In that game, played in Tournament Park in Southern California, Michigan beat Stanford 49–0.

- - - - - - - - - - - - - - - - - - - -*Instant Replay*

Do I know for sure I'm on my way to heaven? If not, whom can I talk to about it?

Sports Stuff

Being prepared is the most important part of being a good athlete. To help yourself be prepared for when you'll get in the game, study the way your favorite athletes conduct themselves. How they respond in tough situations. How they get ready for every play. If you pay attention to really good athletes now, you'll learn great lessons for when you get to higher levels of play.

GAME PLAN

Offer your bodies as living sacrifices, holy and pleasing to God—this is your spiritual act of worship.

Romans 12:1

Play Book Assignment: Read 1 Corinthians 12:1–7

Give It Up for the Coach

What are these students thinking?

It's 6:00 in the morning, and a bunch of swimmers are standing there at the pool, ready to jump in. Is this a polar-bear swim or something?

No, it's the high school swim team, and the shivering students are getting ready for practice. While you're curled up under the blankets, dreaming about getting a good grade in math (dream on), these guys and girls are jumping into that water and swimming their legs off.

Let's say it gets to be 7:30 and they're still swimming. Their muscles ache. Their fingers are all shriveled up. And they know they've got a whole day of classes ahead. Just when they think it's over, the coach yells, "Okay, team, give me ten more laps."

And you know what? Even though they'd rather eat raw fish than swim another stroke, they do it. They flail those tired arms, and they splash their way wearily through those extra laps.

That's because athletes are "living sacrifices" (Romans 12:1). When they show up for practice, they're saying, "Hey, Coach, do with me what you want. Work me. Teach me. Yell at me. Wear me out. I'm yours." They give themselves up for the team.

Are they crazy? What makes them do this?

They realize it's the only way they can be any good. You don't think the Chicago Bulls got as good as they were in the nineties by sitting in front of a big-screen TV eating french fries, do you? No, they worked, sweated, strained, grunted, and groaned. They gave it up for Phil Jackson, their coach.

That's what Paul was talking about in Romans 12:1. He was saying that we should say to God, "Here I am. I'm giving it all up for you."

Do you think you could do that for God? Could you ever say, "God, do with me what you want. Send me to Iceland if you want to. I'll do whatever it takes to give my life to you." That's a true living sacrifice.

Look at what else Paul said. He called giving ourselves up to God our "spiritual act of worship." That makes it ten times better than any sacrifice you'll ever give a coach. You have to respect your coach and listen to him or her, but you're sure not going to worship that person. When we give God our lives, we're telling him, "You are worth worshipping."

He is, don't you think?

On the Chalkboard

Everything of me that I keep for myself is something God can't use.

Speaking of Going All Out

During the 1998 baseball season, Turner Ward of the Pittsburgh Pirates ran through the outfield wall chasing a fly ball. Now that's giving it up!

— — — — — — — — — — — — — — — — — — -*Instant Replay*

What is one thing I can sacrifice, or give up, for God?

Sports Stuff

What did I do today to make myself a better athlete? The best athletes always look for ways to make themselves better. Should I start running or doing push-ups or sit-ups? If I'm not able to do that kind of stuff, what can I do to better myself in some other area of life?

GAME PLAN

> Whatever you do, work at it with all your heart, as working for the Lord, not for men.
>
> Colossians 3:23

Play Book Assignment: Read Philippians 3:12—21

Don't Quit

If you had a choice between flying a plane in the air force or playing football for the Dallas Cowboys, you'd probably pick ...

Tough choice: either strap yourself into the cockpit of a plane that rips through the atmosphere at Mach 2 or strap on a helmet and play football for the most celebrated team in NFL history. (Girls can play this wishing game too, you know. You know there are women pilots, and lots of girls—including soccer star Michelle Akers, who wanted to grow up to play for the Steelers—have football dreams.)

One person never had to make the choice between flying high and blocking low. He got to do both.

His name is Chad Hennings, and he played on the offensive line for the Cowboys in Super Bowls XXVII, XXVIII, and XXX (that's twenty-seven, twenty-eight, and thirty if you're not up on your Roman numerals).

When Chad was in college, he went to the Air Force Academy. That meant that after he graduated, he was obligated to stay in the air force for several more years. For a player who was drafted by the NFL, that meant only one thing. Trouble.

While everyone else who was drafted signed fat contracts and spent their time battling it out in front of tens of thousands of people, Chad was stuck on some air force base somewhere. One of the things he did during that time was to fly the Warthog—a plane that carried supplies to people near Iraq.

Because of his great athletic talent, Chad might have been able to worm his way out of being in the service. But he didn't. When he was a kid his parents taught him that once you start something, you don't quit. And he wasn't about to quit the US Air Force.

Eventually, after fulfilling his obligation, he was able to join the Cowboys.

How are you at sticking to a job you've been given? Do you get about a third of the way through an assignment and then give up on it? Do you start writing a book report and stop after five minutes with terminal writer's cramp? Do you take so long to wash the dishes that the water is cold by the time you're finally done?

There's a way to do better. It starts with remembering that in everything we do, we'll do it better if we do it for God and his glory. When we do that, we can't possibly quit—because that wouldn't please God at all.

Whether you're a big football player like Chad or a little guy who is just struggling to get his science homework done, don't quit. God's depending on you.

> ### On the Chalkboard
> **Serve God with your whole heart, and you won't have anything left to serve the Devil.**

Speaking of Commitment

The NBA player who played the most consecutive games without sitting one out was A.C. Green, a strong Christian. In 1998, he played in his 930th straight game. In 1987, he got two teeth knocked out in a game but still came back to play the next night.

- - - - - - - - - - - - - - - - - - - -Instant Replay

How does completing a job I started bring glory to God?

Sports Stuff

How committed am I to being good at what I do? Would it help to set some goals for how much I should practice? (For example, hit fifty shots every day in basketball; make fifty practice putts a day in golf.) Perhaps I could chart my practice on a piece of paper for a week and then a month and then longer.

> In everything set . . . an example by doing what is good.
>
> Titus 2:7

Play Book Assignment: Read 1 Corinthians 10:31—11:1

Tell a Teammate

Mark Price was one of the best free-throw shooters in NBA history. When he finished his career in 1998, he retired with a career percentage of .904. This means that for every hundred free throws he took in a game, he made ninety of them.

But that wasn't the greatest thing he did as a player in the NBA. No, the best thing he ever did was to live such an impressive life that one of his teammates became a Christian because of it.

While a member of the Cleveland Cavaliers, Price had a teammate named Craig Ehlo. Ehlo and Price became friends. The more Craig watched Mark, the more he noticed that there was something really good about him (besides his shooting ability).

Finally, Mark and his wife, Laura, asked Craig and his wife, Jani, to visit their home. That evening, Mark said, "Craig, if you were to die tonight, do you know if you would go to heaven?"

Because Craig trusted Mark, he took the question seriously, and that night he became a Christian. He prayed to put his faith in Jesus Christ.

Do you think your example can make a difference to others? Are friends, who don't know Jesus like you do, watching to see what kind of person you are? You might think they just want to know if you can hit a baseball or catch a football or shoot free throws. But more important, they're watching to see if what you say about being a Christian is the real deal.

Think about all the things you do with your friends throughout a day. You sit in class with them. You play ball with them. You talk on the phone with them. You hang out at each other's houses. You ride bikes together. How many times during all of those hours together do you think about whether you are being a good example? It's not an easy thing to do.

That's why you have to ask God to help you be a good example. Not a Goody Two-shoes who tells everyone how righteous you are. Not a person who goes around telling everyone how bad they are. Just a dependable friend who keeps doing what's right.

Like Mark Price, be a good example. That's more effective than a 90 percent shooting average.

On the Chalkboard

The best thing you can do for a friend is to introduce him or her to your Best Friend.

Speaking of Example

Mark Price has a little brother whose name is Brent. Brent grew up to play in the NBA, just like Mark. One year, Brent set the NBA record for the most three-pointers in one game—thirteen.

- - - - - - - - - - - - - - - - - - -*Instant Replay*

If my friends were looking at me for an example, would they see Jesus in the way I act? Why? Why not?

Sports Stuff

What's the secret to good free-throw shooting? Three things: balance, shooting position, and release. Keep your legs about shoulder-width apart and bend your knees for balance. Get finger-pad control of the ball (don't let it touch the heel of your hand), bring it to the U position (upper arm parallel to the floor, forearm straight up and down, and hand pulled back parallel to upper arm), and then release with a flick of the wrist as the arm is extended. Your index finger should be pointing toward the basket in your follow-through.

GAME PLAN

[Jesus said] Everyone who hears these words of mine and puts them into practice is like a wise man who built his house on the rock.

Matthew 7:24

Play Book Assignment: Read Matthew 7:24–27

How Embarrassing!

Have you ever dreamed of playing in the World Series? Imagine yourself playing second base in front of fifty thousand screaming people. Just as your team looks as if it's going to give up the losing run on a base hit, you dive through the air, snag a line shot headed for center field, and turn it into a triple play. Your team wins and you are carried off the field in celebration.

Then your mom wakes you up and reminds you to get up and go to school. Bummer.

Tony Fernandez grew up in the Dominican Republic dreaming of playing in the World Series, and he made it. However, his dream turned into something far worse than waking up and having to go to school. He made an error in the 1997 World Series that some say caused his team to lose the series. Tony was playing for the Cleveland Indians, who were favored to beat the Florida Marlins.

Late in the final game of the series, Tony let a ball go through his legs, enabling the Marlins to score and tie the game. If he had caught the ground ball, the Indians probably would have been the world champions.

Most people would have pouted and blamed the ball or the infield. They would have said the ball hit a rock or the lights were too bright or the moon was in the wrong place in the sky. Tony, who is a Christian, didn't do that. He made no excuses. He took full responsibility and talked about what God was teaching him through the problem.

"I don't want to make any excuses," he said about the game. "Jesus says that when disaster strikes, if your life is founded on the Rock [Jesus Christ], it won't be shaken — it doesn't matter how hard the wind blows or the rain falls." He was referring to Matthew 7:24–27.

Tony had things in the right order. He put his life in order a long time before he ran into a problem. As the verses in Matthew say, Tony had built his house on the Rock. A little "rain" wasn't going to wash away his faith.

When you're living for Jesus, you can handle anything. Even embarrassment.

On the Chalkboard

Making excuses is worse than making mistakes. Mistakes can be forgiven; excuses cannot.

Speaking of Embarrassing

During a major-league game a few years ago, an outfielder caught a fly ball in the outfield near the stands. He thought it was the third out, so he flipped the ball to a fan. Oops. It was just the second out, and the runner on third tagged up and scored.

- - - - - - - - - - - - - - - - - - -*Instant Replay*

If I stumble or do something totally uncool, how does it help to have a good relationship with Jesus?

Sports Stuff

When he was a kid growing up in San Pedro de Macoris, Dominican Republic, Tony Fernandez decided he wanted to be a major leaguer. What sports dream do you have? What do you have to do to reach that goal? Should you write that goal out and put it someplace permanent?

Remind the people to be subject to rulers
and authorities, to be obedient, to be ready
to do whatever is good, to slander no one.

Titus 3:1–2

Play Book Assignment: Read 2 Kings 2:19–25

What's in a Name?

What's the most famous nickname you know about in sports?

"Magic" is pretty well known for Earvin "Magic" Johnson. He was one of the best NBA players ever.

"Shaq" is not a small building, but Shaquille O'Neal.

"Big Mac" is not just a burger; it's home-run giant Mark McGwire.

And "The Bus" is not what you take to school; it's Jerome Bettis, the massive NFL running back.

Nicknames can be really fun. Some people get them from their friends or their brothers and sisters, and they last their whole lives.

But there's another kind of nickname that isn't as much fun. It's the nickname you get from people who aren't very nice. Like the kid who gets the name "Shorty" hung on him even though it embarrasses him. Or when cruel kids call someone "Chubby" or "Four Eyes" or "Dumbo."

These aren't nicknames that anyone wants, and we have to be careful not to call people by names that will hurt their feelings.

As you might guess, there's not much in the Bible about nicknames, but there is one incident when some people tried to insult a man with a nickname. It was in 2 Kings 2:23. God's prophet Elisha was walking toward Bethel when a bunch of kids who didn't care that Elisha was God's special messenger started yelling at him. "Go on up, you baldhead!" they screamed at him. They were mocking him not necessarily because he was hairless but because he was on God's side.

Sometimes that might happen to you. You might get dubbed a "church girl" or a "Goody Two-shoes" because you stick up for what you think is right. On the other hand, you might find yourself thinking it's clever to give another kid a mean nickname.

If someone tries to nail you with an embarrassing nickname, the best thing to do is to stay calm about it. The verse that says "A gentle answer turns away wrath" (Proverbs 15:1) helps you know how to respond. And it helps you know to avoid being on the giving end of nasty talk, because it also says, "a harsh word stirs up anger."

Nothing wrong with nicknames—as long as they don't make you or the person who is given one feel bad. Use them and give them carefully.

On the Chalkboard
A nickname that hurts is a nickname that should never be given.

Speaking of Nicknames

The most common college nickname for a school team is Eagles, claimed by forty-seven schools. One of the weirdest is Banana Slug. One school has that nickname: the University of California at Santa Cruz.

- - - - - - - - - - - - - - - - - - -*Instant Replay*

If I've ever called anyone by a not-so-nice nickname, why did I do that? Did it make me feel powerful? Do I need to apologize?

Sports Stuff

One of the most famous basketball players ever had the nickname Pistol Pete. What was his last name? He had the highest scoring average ever in college basketball. He averaged more than forty-four points a game when he was a senior at LSU. There was only one way he could get that good. He practiced basketball constantly. He even took a ball to bed with him. Try this Pete Maravich (that's his name) trick: dribble a basketball while riding your bike (wear your helmet).

> If you falter in times of trouble, how small is your strength!
>
> Proverbs 24:10

Play Book Assignment: Read Luke 5:1–11

I Won't Run . . .

Harold Abrahams was ticked.

He had just run an early heat in the 100-meter dash, and he stunk. It was the Olympic Games of 1924 (yes, they had Olympic Games back then), and Harry was expected to win the 100-meter dash. He ran well enough to qualify for the finals, but he felt terrible about his race.

He was so disgusted with himself that after he finished his heat, he walked over to where his fiancée was sitting, sat down, and told her, "I won't run anymore if I can't win."

Guys, one day you'll understand how wise girls can be. Harry Abrahams sure found out how smart his favorite young woman was that day. He probably expected her to hold his hand and say, "Yes, Harry. You're right. That's just what I'd do."

She didn't do anything of the kind. She looked over at her sweaty husband-to-be and said to him, "If you don't run, you can't win."

If the expression "Well, duh!" had been popular back then, that would have worked too. Her statement was brilliant yet simple.

Instead of agreeing that he should quit because of a small setback, she was telling him, "Go for it! You can't win if you don't try."

Harry listened to his lady and proceeded to go out on the track, set an Olympic record, and win the Olympic gold in the 100-meter race.

Often we want to be successful at being the kind of person God wants us to be, but we mess up. Then we decide to give up. We stop before God has a chance to help us do what he wants us to do.

Peter ran into that problem out on the Sea of Galilee. He was having a bad night fishing and was ready to quit. Then Jesus gave him a pointer, and he netted more fish than he could handle. Just think what he would have missed if he had quit (Luke 5: 1–9).

Okay, what does God want you to do? Better start working on it. You can't get it done by just sitting there.

On the Chalkboard

If at first you don't succeed, it might be because you didn't try at all.

Speaking of the 1924 Olympics

Another runner in the 1924 Olympics was Eric Liddell. He refused to run on Sunday in his best race because he felt it wouldn't honor God. He then registered for the 400-meter run, which he won. His story is told in the movie *Chariots of Fire*. After the Olympics, Liddell became a missionary to China.

- - - - - - - - - - - - - - - - - - - -*Instant Replay*

Last week I failed at _____,
and I was afraid to give it another try until now.
Tomorrow I will be successful at it,
and even if I'm not I'll keep trying.

Sports Stuff

List three sports skills you know you need to improve on (dribbling a soccer ball, shooting layups, stengthening your golf swing — something like that). In the next two weeks, repeat this skill at least one hundred times a day to improve.

GAME PLAN

[Jesus] himself bore our sins in his body on the tree, so that we might die to sins and live for righteousness; by his wounds you have been healed.

1 Peter 2:24

Play Book Assignment: Read Ephesians 2:1–10

What Salvation Is For

Rosalynn Sumners was really mad at God.

She thought he had let her down big-time.

Rosalynn had spent almost her entire life working to be one of the best figure skaters in the world. In fact, when she was nineteen years old, nearly everyone expected her to become the best in the world. She went to the 1984 Olympics knowing that if she didn't win the gold medal, she would be a disappointment to many people.

At the games, which were held in Sarajevo, Yugoslavia, Rosalynn skated with her heart and with all the skill she could muster. When the points were added up, she had finished second to Katarina Witt of East Germany. Rosalynn had come within one tenth of one point of winning the gold. Tears of disappointment streamed down her face as she stood on the podium and received her silver medal.

Although Rosalynn Sumners had put her faith in Jesus Christ earlier in her life, when she didn't win the gold medal, she got very angry with God.

For the next ten years, she didn't want anything to do with him. During this time, she made a lot of money as a professional skater, and millions of people across America cheered for her. She smiled and skated and waved and acted as if she was the happiest person on blades.

But she wasn't happy. In 1995, though, she and a friend played a CD by a Christian rock group called Stryper. As she listened to the CD, Rosalynn was suddenly touched by a Bible verse on the CD cover. It said, "By his stripes we are healed."

Right away, Rosalynn realized that she had turned her back on Jesus, who died for her. She recalled that his wounds had healed her heart. The anger went away, and she began to thank God for what he had done.

Sometimes we think that God is in our lives to make life easier. That if we trust him we'll have enough money to go to the mall. That it's his job to help us get good grades or make the soccer team. That the reason he died for us was to make everything go smoothly.

While it's true that our Lord is involved in our lives and that he does want what is best for us, the most important thing Jesus does for us is save us from the penalty of our sin. We are "alive with Christ" (Ephesians 2:5). That's the really, really good news.

No matter what bad things happen, we need to stick close to Jesus, our Savior. Blaming him for our bad breaks and then running from him will just get us into bigger trouble.

On the Chalkboard

The power that makes our hearts right is strong enough to help us when things go wrong.

Olympic Note

The most medals won by an Olympic athlete is eighteen by Larisa Latynina of the former USSR. A gymnast, Latynina won six medals in each of the 1956, 1960, and 1964 Olympic Games.

-Instant Replay

When things get tough for me, is it easier to tell God thanks for my salvation or to blame him for my problems? What is one thing I can thank God for today?

Sports Stuff

Give it a try. Rosalynn Sumners first tried skating when she was seven years old because her mom had a coupon for free skating at a local rink. Rosalynn liked it! Are you willing to try a new sport? Some kids don't know they can do a sport—and think they can't—until they get out there and try.

> But seek first [God's] kingdom and his righ-
> teousness, and all these things will be given
> to you as well.
>
> Matthew 6:33

Play Book Assignment: Read Matthew 6:25–34

Hold On, but Not Too Tight

In the history of women's soccer, a couple of names stand out. One is Mia Hamm. She's probably the most famous star. The other is Michelle Akers, the woman who was the first female soccer player to be called the best in the world.

Michelle was a member of the 1991 and the 1999 US National teams that won the World Cup of soccer. She is known as the kind of player who would run through a brick wall if it would help her team win. And she's been that kind of player since she was about seven years old, first playing in Seattle, Washington.

But between 1991 and 1999, Michelle had a huge fight on her hands just to be able to play soccer. For one thing, she suffered from about a dozen knee injuries that required surgery. For another, she had a disease called chronic fatigue and immune dysfunction syndrome (CFIDS). This disease makes Michelle feel tired all the time. Some days she hardly has the strength to get out of bed.

Michelle is a Christian who trusted Jesus as her Savior while she was an all-American soccer player in high school. However, she stopped living for Christ while in college. Her entire life was wrapped up in soccer.

After the United States won the World Cup in 1991, however, she recognized that her life was empty. She had fame and money, but she wasn't happy.

She realized that her life was falling apart because she wasn't the kind of Christian she should be. So she rededicated her life to Jesus.

That didn't mean her troubles were over. In fact, her physical troubles increased. Yet she never turned her back on God again. She realized that she needed to trust him as she went through her struggles.

Today as she looks back, she says, "God gave me back my soccer, as long as I hold it loosely." Now she puts God first, and she is happier than she's ever been.

Even when you're young, you can allow stuff other than God to get too important. It could be friends. Or sports. Or … well, you know what you struggle with.

As Michelle did, let God be number one in your life. It'll help you enjoy life's other good things even more.

On the Chalkboard

**When we hold on to stuff too tightly,
it soon gets hold of us.**

Sports Note

In 1999, Michelle Akers was named the women's soccer Player of the Century.

------------------- -*Instant Replay*

**What's starting to become more important to me than God?
Music? Friends? My computer? Is there anything I can
do to avoid the sadness Michelle had in her life?**

Sports Stuff

One of the best ways to get better at your sport is to play against people who are better or bigger or stronger than you. When Michelle Akers was your age, she played soccer against guys. The University of Tennessee women's basketball team practices against guys every day. Don't practice against people you can beat; practice against people you can learn from.

An anxious heart weighs a man down, but a kind word cheers him up.

Proverbs 12:25

Play Book Assignment: Read 1 Timothy 3:6–10

Way to Go!

Do you know anyone who runs marathons? My brother has run them. He has even run in the Boston Marathon, which is the most famous one in the world. To him, it was the highlight of his running career. To me, it would be twenty-six miles and 385 yards of self-inflicted torture. Why, I used to think, would anybody, or in the case of the Boston Marathon, thousands of anybodies, run that far? For fun.

Wouldn't it be easier just to light fire to your shoes and whack yourself in the leg with a ball bat? Wouldn't that create the same end result?

Well, I've learned some things that have changed my thinking. I began to find out a little more about running long distances when my daughter began running cross-country in high school. I discovered, for one thing, that people who run cross-country get a lot of encouragement. From everybody.

Have you ever been to a race—either a cross-country race or a marathon? It's so very different from the sports I'm used to—basketball, baseball, and football.

At ball games, fans yell *at* people, for the most part. "Hey, Number 10. Can't you dribble any better than that?" Or "Yo, Ref! Did you miss that foul on purpose, or are you blind?"

At running events, fans yell *for* people. "Nice job, Mike! Way to run!" "Go, Rachel! You're doin' great!"

For some reason, a major part of running sports is that people go to the events to help the runners feel good about what they are doing. Some go to hand out water. Others just cheer. But no one goes and hollers, "Hey, Number 1395. My grandmother runs better than that!" So one reason people run, I guess, is because other people like to shout encouraging things to them.

When it comes to how you treat your friends, your parents, and your classmates, are you like a cross-country fan or a ball-game fan? Are you encouraging them or making them feel like day-old roadkill? Do you make positive comments that build people up, or do you say negative, nasty things?

Look at the encouraging report the apostle Paul gave in 1 Thessalonians 3. Imagine how good this report made everyone—Paul, Timothy, and the people in Thessalonica—feel.

If saying "Way to go!" helps people run twenty-six miles, maybe telling a friend "You are special" will make her day.

Maybe if handing out a cup of water to a thirsty runner helps him run faster, imagine what you can do for someone in your class by doing something good for him or her.

On the Chalkboard

A word of encouragement speaks volumes about the kind of person you are.

Sports History Note

The first marathon was run in 1896 at the first Olympic Games of the modern era. (The last Olympics before that was held in AD 393.) The original distance was 24.85 miles, which was the distance a Greek messenger, named Pheidippides, ran in 490 BC from the Plain of Marathon to Athens, Greece, to tell his people that the Greeks had defeated the Persian army. The current distance of 26 miles 385 yards was agreed upon in 1924.

- -*Instant Replay*

Would I consider myself an encourager or a criticizer? Whom can I encourage today?

Sports Stuff

How far can you run? You might surprise yourself. Why not map out some distances in your neighborhood (a half mile, mile, mile and a half) and test yourself. It's great exercise, and you might end up being a cross-country star. One goal is to run 3.1 miles, or 5K. That's the distance for high school cross-country. Want a goal for 5K? Try less than twenty-five minutes.

Day 11

The testing of your faith develops perseverance.

James 1:3

Play Book Assignment: Read 2 Timothy 2:1–3

Don't You Ever Win?

In 1996, a young woman from Detroit, Michigan, made a name for herself by winning a gold medal in the Olympic Games in Atlanta. You may have never heard of her, but this remarkable person's name is Sheila Taormina.

Sheila had tried out for the 1992 Olympics but didn't make the team. And even her selection to the 1996 team wasn't easy. In fact, she was the last person to make the squad. And she was allowed to compete in the 4 x 200–meter swimming race only because someone else had been disqualified.

What makes Sheila truly remarkable, though, is her attitude toward life after she won the gold medal. Suddenly she was famous, and people all across the country wanted to see her and hear her speak. So she tried to make everyone happy. Any time someone called to ask her to come to their event, she did.

And she took her gold medal with her. As she would tell her story, she would let the people in the audience handle that precious disk. She would do this even when she spoke in elementary schools. More than once, kids would drop or in some other way mistreat her prize possession. Sheila would just go on telling her stories.

Part of the story she told her listeners was the difficulty she had in making the US swim team. Sheila would tell of all the times she didn't qualify or all the times she didn't win, trying to let the kids know that it's okay to fail as long as you keep trying.

One time, as Sheila told her story, a little girl began to cry. Noticing this, Sheila put her arm around her and said, "Did I say something to upset you?"

With tears on her face and her big eyes turned toward Sheila, the little girl sniffed and said, "Didn't you ever win?"

You know what? Losing is sad. It's not easy to keep going when you don't get what you want.

But we can learn from Sheila. Physically, she wouldn't quit. And spiritually neither should we. God wants us to hang tough (persevere) and trust him when things are hard. That's what Paul meant when he said, "Endure hardship" (2 Timothy 2:3).

Let's say you're struggling to read your Bible every day. If you miss a couple of days, don't quit. Start again. Or maybe you have a friend who isn't a Christian, and you want to witness to him or her. But then you slip and say something you shouldn't, and you feel like you've let God down. Paul gave you the answer. He said, "Be strong in the grace that is in Christ Jesus" (2 Timothy 2:1). You can trust that God is with you, and you can gain strength in Jesus's love.

Sometimes you might look at yourself and say, "Don't you ever win?" Just look back and say, "Jesus and I can do anything." Then go for the victory.

On the Chalkboard

You and Jesus are a winning combination.

Sports History Note

If you have trouble swimming from one side of the pool to the other, it'll be hard to believe what Gustave Brickner did. The Pennsylvania native, who kept track of how much he swam in a lifetime, covered 38,512 miles of water in his fifty-nine years of swimming.

- - - - - - - - - - - - - - - - - - -*Instant Replay*

Do I feel like a winner or a loser? If a loser, how can Jesus help me?

Sports Stuff

After her Olympic career in swimming was over, Sheila didn't stop competing. She became a triathlete: swimming, biking, running. Many athletes use cross-training as a way to get better. Could cross-training help you in your favorite sport?

GAME PLAN

I [wisdom] love those who love me,

and those who seek me find me.

Proverbs 8:17

Play Book Assignment: Read Deuteronomy 10:12−21

Who's First?

Here's the perfect sport for you: triathlon.

Think about it. You like to ride a bike, don't you? And during the summer, you love to swim, right?

Well, there is that little thing about running, but hey, you run to the fridge all the time during the commercials, so how bad can this be?

Triathlon is a sport that combines all three of those really fun ways to exercise: biking, swimming, running.

One of the best women triathletes in the world is Barb Lindquist. She lives in Wyoming, and she loves training for this sport. During 1999, she even won an award as the US National Champion in the triathlon.

As a follower of Jesus Christ, Barb uses her fame as a great athlete to tell others about her Savior. And she tries to keep the most important things in her life in the order in which they should be.

Here's how things should be, according to Barb:

First priority: God

Second priority: her husband, Loren

Third priority: her sport, triathlon

She has a pretty good checklist for making sure she's doing things right. If any of these things start getting out of whack—for instance, if she puts running before God—she knows it's time to do some rearranging.

The best time to start developing this kind of priority list is right now. When you're young. When you have a lot fewer things to keep in order.

One day, you'll have a car, a spouse, a house, a job, money, friends, responsibilities at church, and other stuff. These things will all beg for your attention. It'll be really easy to end up having God be about number eight on your list.

So now, when your life is a little simpler and you have fewer things in the way, why not make it a point to put God at the top. Here's your own checklist:

1. Did I talk to God this morning before I talked to anyone else?
2. Did I ask God to help me throughout the day?
3. Did I look at God's message to me in the Bible, or did I have a bunch of other things that were more important?
4. Did I let anyone else know that God is important in my life?

Checking on these things will help you do as Moses said: "Fear the Lord, . . . walk in all his ways, . . . love him, . . . serve

[him]" (Deuteronomy 10:12). It'll help you keep in mind "Who's first?"

On the Chalkboard

For a relationship with God that will last, put him first.

Sports History Note

The sport of triathlon began in 1978 when two men challenged each other to a contest of 2.4 miles swimming, 112 miles biking, and 26 miles 385 yards running. Two years later, the race had 108 competitors and was televised on ABC-TV.

- - - - - - - - - - - - - - - - - - - -*Instant Replay*

Some wear a WWJD or PUSH bracelet to remind themselves of the importance of God in their lives. Here's what I plan to do:

_____

Sports Stuff

Mom says, "You need to do some running and get in shape." Before you take off, remember this tip: it is always best to warm up a little before doing your stretching exercises. Stretching while your muscles are cold could lead to muscle tears.

> Above all else, guard your heart.
>
> Proverbs 4:23

Play Book Assignment: Read Ephesians 5:1–11

Be Your Own Goalie!

Imagine playing hockey without a goalkeeper.

Once in a while it happens. At the end of some hockey games, a team that is behind will pull its goalie off the ice and put in another offensive player so they have a better chance to score a goal.

And sometimes when that happens, it backfires. Instead of the team with the extra man scoring, the team with the open net will send one across the ice and watch it slide untouched into the net. It's an empty-netter, and it counts just as much as the one Brett Hull sneaked by Dominik Hašek in game seven of the 1999 Stanley Cup finals. (Well, maybe not quite as much, since it's not for the Stanley Cup. But it's still a goal.)

Did you know it's possible to live your life with an empty net? It can happen when you don't know how to stop bad influences from sneaking into your life—when you let them in just like a Wayne Gretzky slap shot flying into the back of an unattended net.

That's why you need to strap on the pads and learn to play goalie. Not on the hockey ice, but in your life. You need to stand your ground against any kind of influence that might damage you.

For instance, when you hear someone start to tell a dirty joke or when you get the urge to watch something on TV that you know is wrong, you need to guard the goal. You need to "guard your heart," as the writer of Proverbs said (4:23). Every day, there are dozens of ways you can fill your heart with things that will harm you, so it's important to protect yourself.

The apostle Paul said we should imitate God. And one thing we know for sure about God is that he hates sin. Just as a hockey goalkeeper will do anything he can to stop that dreaded puck from getting into his net, so we have to protect our hearts from anything that will separate us from God.

How are your goalkeeping skills?

On the Chalkboard

You can't stop sin by pretending it's okay; you have to hate it.

Sports History Note

In 1949, goalie Bill Durnan of the National Hockey League's Montreal Canadiens shut out the Canadiens' opponents for

309 straight minutes. His string of shutout hockey extended across parts of six games and included four straight complete-game shutouts.

- - - - - - - - - - - - - - - - - - - -*Instant Replay*

A goalie has gloves, pads, and a stick to protect the goal. What are my tools? How often do I use them?

Sports Stuff

When we talk about goaltenders, we're talking defense. Sometimes, young athletes don't like to talk about, or play, defense. The glory is in scoring, they think. But keep in mind that you can win a lot of points with a coach if you show him or her that you are willing to play good defense. Study good defenders in your sport and watch how they get the edge. No one wins without a good defense. Someday, maybe you can be the key to your team's defense.

Consequently, you are no longer foreigners and aliens, but fellow citizens.

Ephesians 2:19

Play Book Assignment: Read Ephesians 2:19—22

Heart Friends

Let's say you go to summer camp and meet someone who lives four hundred miles away. This person goes to a different school, lives in a different region of the country, has different interests, and even roots for a different team in the NBA.

This person may even be a different color, go to a different kind of church, and have a totally different family situation. Almost everything about you two is different. Well, maybe you both have a dog.

This person can't be your friend, right? Isn't this other camper so unlike you that you wouldn't have anything to share?

But wait. You find out this faraway person is a Christian. He or she loves Jesus just like you do. Suddenly, everything changes. Just like that, you have a reason to like this person a lot. You start to feel like this person's friend.

Something like that happened to Michelle Akers, star soccer player for the US women's team in the 1999 World Cup. As the US team prepared to play China for the championship, Michelle, who is a strong Christian, heard that the goalie for the Chinese team was also a follower of Jesus Christ.

So as the two teams passed each other in the tunnel going out onto the field at the Rose Bowl, Michelle looked for the Chinese goalie. She knew they couldn't communicate in words, so when Michelle saw Gao Hong, she pointed toward her heart and then pointed to heaven. The woman from China saw the gesture, broke into a smile, and did the same thing.

Just like that, two women from two different cultures realized that they had the greatest bond in the world. They both loved Jesus.

Think about your Christian friends. Do you feel you have a special bond? That you are more than friends?

Look at what the apostle Paul said in Ephesians. He said you and your friends are "members of God's household" (2:19). Of course, you're not going to run over to them tomorrow, hug them, and say, "I love you!" But you can in your own quiet way appreciate what God has done by giving you people who are more than acquaintances. They are friends from the heart.

God did something pretty special when he made all Christians brothers and sisters.

On the Chalkboard

There is no greater friend than a
friend who loves Jesus.

Sports History Note

In 1988, twenty-two students from Roy High School in Roy,
Utah, played a soccer game that lasted 75 ½ hours.

------------------------*Instant Replay*

**What difference does it makes when I have a friend who
shares my faith? Who is one friend like that, and how
does it make the friendship special?**

Sports Stuff

Do you play soccer? If so, have you ever set a goal (no pun
intended) to try at least fifty shots on goal a day? Or to see if
you can dribble a ball in the air for three minutes? Or to practice heading for five minutes a day? Set some goals and see if
you don't improve your ball handling skills.

What is your life? You are a mist that appears for a little while and then vanishes.

James 4:14

Play Book Assignment: Read 2 Corinthians 5:16—6:2

How Much Time Left?

The first game for the United States in the 1994 World Cup of Soccer was held at the Silverdome, the home of the Detroit Lions.

My family and I were there for an exciting game between the US team and Switzerland. As the game wound down toward the ninetieth minute, the score was tied at 2–2. Of course, the US fans were screaming and yelling for the Americans to put one more goal in the net as the teams frantically tried to move the ball.

Finally, the clocks in the Silverdome reached the ninety-minute mark. But the game didn't stop. The teams played on as the referee on the field became the only person in the stadium who knew how much time was left. He had kept track of all injury and substitution time-outs, and he alone knew if there were two minutes left or five.

It was weird as a fan to sit there and not know if there was time for the US to score. Those were some tense minutes as the teams battled without knowing when the game would be over.

Finally, the ref blew his whistle, and the game ended at 2−2.

Life is like that soccer rule. There is only one Person who knows when our final whistle will blow and we will have to account for ourselves before him. That Person is God.

As a young person, you probably don't think much about dying. You're enjoying life too much. And besides, only really old people die, right?

Sadly, that's not true. Nothing in this life guarantees that you have any longer than a typical "extra time" period in soccer. Our lives are totally in God's hands.

The Bible says that our lives are kind of like a mist that is here one minute and *poof!* gone the next (James 4:14). In that little "mist" time, God asks us to commit our lives to him through Jesus Christ.

It's not any fun to think about the fact that we don't know if we'll be here tomorrow, but it's important. God wants each of us to be ready to meet him. He wants us to make sure we have a personal relationship with him through faith in Jesus Christ.

And only God knows when our time is up.

On the Chalkboard

When life's final moment arrives, there's no time for a new game plan.

Sports History Note

The men's World Cup of Soccer has been contested since 1930. Brazil has won it four times, while Italy and West Germany (now just Germany) have won it three times. The women's World Cup began in 1991. The US has won it twice (1991 and 1999), while Norway won it in 1995.

- - - - - - - - - - - - - - - - - - -*Instant Replay*

Do I know for sure that I have put my faith in Jesus Christ?

Sports Stuff

If you want to be ready at the end of a soccer match to take advantage of "stoppage time," you have to be in shape. You may have already played ninety minutes, but the game goes on. That's why it's important to work hard at conditioning. Some soccer players don't take conditioning seriously, either before the season or during practice. If you want an advantage over everyone else, then train harder than everyone else. That will help you overcome weak spots in your game.

Prepare your minds for action.

1 Peter 1:13

Play Book Assignment: Read 1 Peter 1:13–21

What Are You Going to Do?

There's a runner on first and second. There is one out. The batter is left-handed, and he doesn't run very fast. Your team is ahead by one run in the last inning. It's a home game.

Your pitcher has the ball and is getting ready to pitch. You're standing at shortstop with your hands on your knees.

What are you thinking about? How nice your uniform looks? What Mom is cooking for supper? How blue the sky is? What it's going to be like to go swimming after the game? What you're going to feel like when you get your gold medal in the 2016 Olympics?

It better not be any of those things.

You're supposed to be deciding what you're going to do if the ball is hit to you. Or what you do if it goes to a teammate.

One of the most important principles in baseball or softball is to know ahead of time what you're going to do when the play begins. Every time your pitcher throws the ball, you're supposed to know already what you're going to do in any situation that might come up. Why? Because once the ball is in play again, you won't have time to make a lot of decisions.

Now let's leave the game behind and talk about life in the real world. Same principle applies. The key to success is to think ahead of time about all the possible situations. Then, when stuff happens, you're ready.

Here's how Peter said it in 1 Peter 1:13: "Prepare your minds for action."

For instance, you're talking to a friend, and he says, "My dad says there ain't no God."

Or you're at the mall, and the person you're with says, "Look at this shirt. I think I can get it out of here without paying."

Or you're at church, and one of your leaders says, "Would you be willing to read a verse and talk about it next week during our after-church Share and Care?"

Or you're walking home from school, and a guy walks by, shoves some drugs in your hand, and says, "Here, kid. Try this."

Do you think you're ready for these situations?

Once the ball is hit to you, it's too late to come up with a plan.

On the Chalkboard
Failing to plan is planning to fail.

Sports History Note

There was little time for indecision on August 30, 1916. On
that day two baseball teams from the Carolina League (a minor
league) played a nine-inning game in thirty-one minutes. It
seems the visiting team from Winston-Salem didn't want to
miss its train, so the manager asked the home team, Asheville,
if they could speed things up. The game began at 1:28 and was
over at 1:59.

- - - - - - - - - - - - - - - - - - -*Instant Replay*

What possible situation worries me? How can I prepare?

Sports Stuff

One way to help yourself prepare is to keep a notebook of sce-
narios in your sport. You can jot stuff down as you watch the
pros play, or you can keep notes of what coaches tell you in
whatever league you play in. For instance, if you play baseball, notice what major-league teams do in bunt situations or
in double-play situations. It'll make the games more fun to
watch, and you'll begin to understand the sport better.

GAME PLAN

In the beginning God created the heavens and the earth.

Genesis 1:1

Play Book Assignment: Read Genesis 1

Who Invented Baseball?

Back in the mid-1800s, people began playing a game called "base ball." It started mostly in the eastern part of the United States before it spread west and then around the world.

There is some disagreement, though, about who invented the game. Some say it came from a game called "rounders" that was played in England. Others say it was cooked up by Abner Doubleday. Still others claim it was created by Alexander Cartwright.

Although it's not clear who first came up with the concept, it's clear that someone did. The game didn't just happen one day. A bunch of people didn't just show up on a vacant lot one afternoon to find pieces of wood that had become bats and hunks of leather and rubber and string that had developed into baseballs. They didn't find a field that was accidentally laid out with bases ninety feet apart and with a pitcher's mound sixty feet six inches from home plate.

No, there was a designer, or several designers, behind it all.

Now let's think about something a lot bigger than a baseball field. Let's think about the universe.

Nobody created it. It just happened. And out of the deadness of this universe, suddenly things started appearing on earth. Things with life in them sprang up. They just developed on their own. Of course, they weren't much. Just little one-celled things. But they started changing into other things, somehow. They didn't have eyes, but they developed them. They didn't have ears, but they soon came along. Then some of them made the jump from little one-celled things to fish or something. And eventually some of them jumped out onto land. Their gills changed in a mysterious way to lungs. And some of them dropped the fin thing and grew feet.

On and on the story goes. Unbelievable, isn't it?

But people believe it.

Baseball was invented; it didn't just appear.

The universe was created; it didn't just appear. God, who has existed forever, made the entire universe. He flung the stars light-years apart. He put the earth in the exact place it needed to be to support life. And he made earth a place of beauty. Then, to top it off, he made all living things, including us.

Ever think about how great God is because he made the world? We honor people all the time for what they invented or discovered or developed. We still remember the inventor of basketball, James Naismith, more than one hundred years later. Thomas Edison, who gave us electric lighting and other things, has several museums in his honor.

But God? He created the whole world and everyone in it.

That ought to make us want to praise him and thank him and worship him. Our Creator-God is awesome!

On the Chalkboard

God's handprints cannot be erased from his creation.

Sports History Note

There are references to "base ball" in the 1700s, long before the game was said to have been invented by either Alexander Cartwright or Abner Doubleday. But it began to be popular in about 1850 or so. The first game on record was played in 1846 in New York.

- - - - - - - - - - - - - - - - - - -Instant Replay

What is the most amazing fact about creation? Should I spend a few minutes thanking God for all he made?

Sports Stuff

Have you ever tried to invent a new game? You might want to think about it. Remember, James Naismith invented basketball by using a volleyball in a different way. So you can use existing items from other sports to create your own contest. Then get some friends together and try it.

> But when you pray, go into your room, close the door and pray to your Father, who is unseen.
>
> Matthew 6:6

Play Book Assignment: Read Matthew 14:22–23; Mark 1:35

A Place to Pray

If your church looked like a shower room, would you go?

For many professional athletes, that's exactly where they go to pray.

Most pro basketball, baseball, and football teams have a chaplain who meets with the players at least once a week, usually on Sunday, to pray and study the Bible. They meet wherever they can find a quiet space away from the noise of a team preparing for a game. And sometimes, the best place to meet is in the shower room. Nobody goes in there *before* the game.

As the season wears on, the players look forward to getting together for chapel because they know they will have a special place to pray. No matter whether it's a training room, a coach's office, or the shower room, this prayer sanctuary helps the players stay in touch with God.

Do you have a special place in your house where you can pray? Imagine how nice it would be to have a place where you go every day to meet with God. Maybe there's a spare room in the basement where people seldom go. Or perhaps your dad's workbench in the garage. Or it could be your own bedroom.

Make it someplace where there is no TV, no radio, no magazines. Put a Bible there and a pad of paper on which you can write down prayer requests. And put up an Off Limits sign when you go there so everyone else in the family knows to leave you alone with God.

When Jesus wanted some special time alone with God, he sometimes went into the hills near Jerusalem. That was his refuge where he could have heart-to-heart talks with the Father. You may not be able to have a place as majestic as a Judean mountain, but that's okay. Jesus suggested that you "go into your room, close the door and pray" (Matthew 6:6).

Developing a prayer place could make a big difference in your relationship with God. You'll find yourself looking forward to getting together with him.

It may not be a shower room or a mountain, but think about finding a place to pray.

On the Chalkboard

When you get alone to pray with God, you're not alone.

Sports Note

Baseball was the first pro sport to have regular chapel services. Baseball Chapel was started by a sportswriter named Watson "Waddy" Spoelstra. In the 1960s, he went to the commissioner of baseball, Bowie Kuhn, and asked for permission to have Sunday services with the players who wanted to attend. Now there are chapel programs in the NFL, the NBA, the WNBA, and Major League Baseball. In 1998, the NHL approved them, and chaplains have been trying to get programs started there as well.

- - - - - - - - - - - - - - - - - - -*Instant Replay*

Okay, where is my prayer room going to be? In the next week, I vow to use the room at least five times.

Sports Stuff

If you have a favorite player and you'd like to write to him or her, send your letter in care of the team for which that athlete plays. You can get a list of team addresses from a couple of sources: *ESPN Sports Almanac* and *A Sports Fan's Guide to Christian Athletes and Sports Trivia* (Moody Press).

> A gentle answer turns away wrath, but a harsh word stirs up anger.
>
> Proverbs 15:1

Play Book Assignment: Read Matthew 5:38–42

Base-Brawl

When people think of home runs and baseball, they usually think of Mark McGwire and Sammy Sosa. But what Kim Braatz did in 1996 is pretty important too.

Of course, Kim's effort didn't get her on the cover of *Sports Illustrated*, and it didn't turn a baseball into a million-dollar piece of memorabilia. But it's still a big deal.

Kim hit the first over-the-fence home run for a team of women baseball players who played against men. She played for a team called the Silver Bullets, which was made up of some really talented women baseball players.

On July 16, 1996, while playing in Cape Cod, Massachusetts, Braatz belted a low fastball over the 315-foot sign in left field to make her mark on history.

That wasn't the only thing Kim did on the baseball field that year that made history. The second thing, however, is something she's not quite as proud of. Well, actually, she's not proud of it at all.

In a different game that season, Kim found herself in the middle of the first fight in women's-men's pro baseball. It seems that the pitcher of an opposing team nailed her with a pitch. That would have been okay, but then he laughed at her as she made her way to first base.

Bad idea. Kim thought her honor as a baseball player was at stake, so she headed out to the mound to settle the score with the pitcher. A fight followed, and Braatz had her second first of the season.

Later, Kim, a strong Christian woman, had second thoughts about the fight. She knew that a lot of people looked up to her because of her faith, and she felt she had let them down. "I shouldn't have done that," she finally concluded. "I should have turned the other cheek." She decided that Jesus wasn't happy with the way she responded.

What she did by reacting incorrectly is no different from what we do when we respond with harsh words or mean comments to something someone says to us. The big difference in Kim's situation was that her act was witnessed by a lot of people, including reporters who sent her story around the country.

Kim learned from her mistake, and she realizes now how harmful anger can be.

Do you struggle with anger? Do you get mad easily if your parents tell you no? Do you fly into a rage if your brother or sister looks at you the wrong way? Do you yell at your teammates if they don't do what you think they should?

Following are a couple of Scripture verses that can really help. But you can't just read them and forget about them. You need to write them on a card and put them where you'll see them. On your bulletin board in your room. In your locker at school. On the bottom of the bill of your baseball cap. Wherever they can remind you of God's method of handling anger.

The first verse is "A gentle answer turns away wrath" (Proverbs 15:1). You can make sure a little problem doesn't get big by answering people calmly and kindly. The second is the one Kim referred to: "If someone strikes you on the right cheek, turn to him the other also" (Matthew 5:39). That means you let some stuff go. You don't fight back. Both verses say that if we want to please God, you'll seek to avoid trouble by your response, not make things worse.

Be careful not to turn someone else's comment into your own version of base-brawl.

On the Chalkboard

If you want to get angry at something, get angry at sin.

Instant Replay

I have a problem with anger.
I don't have a problem with anger.

Which sentence describes me?

If I do, what am I going to do to stop it from causing me problems?

Sports Stuff

You don't have to be huge to hit home runs. Kim Braatz is just five feet seven inches tall. The first secret is having good forearm strength. That was the situation with Hank Aaron, who hit the most home runs ever. He had great forearms. The second secret that will help you hit a baseball or softball farther is bat speed. So, strengthen those forearms and increase the speed of your bat as it moves through the strike zone.

> Jonathan said to David, "Go in peace, for we have sworn friendship with each other in the name of the LORD."
>
> 1 Samuel 20:42

Play Book Assignment: Read 1 Samuel 20:1–17

True Friends

Do you have a friend who is a foot taller than you? Avery Johnson does. His friend's name is David Robinson, and they were both members of the 1999 NBA champion San Antonio Spurs.

Besides being teammates on that title-winning team, the two of them were best buddies. They did stuff together during the off-season. David helped Avery with his computer. (Robinson is a computer expert.) Avery encouraged David to work out in the gym. (Johnson is a gym rat.) And their families hung out together.

But one of the neatest things about their friendship happened in the spring of 1999 when the Spurs were battling to win the NBA Championship. Avery told reporters that he wanted to win the championship more for David than for himself. Wow! That's a friend.

Think about you and your friends. Do you want them to get nice stuff? Do you want them to get good grades? Do you want them to go on the best missions trips? Sometimes it's easier to wish the best for ourselves and be jealous of our friends when things go their way.

David and Avery sound a little like a couple of really good friends in the Old Testament: Jonathan and David. They too had a battle on their hands, but theirs was life-and-death. Jonathan's father was Saul, and he wanted to kill David. Jonathan wanted to stop that from happening. So he and David devised a plan that would save David's life. It was a risky situation for Jonathan because he would be in huge trouble if his dad knew he was helping David. Yet he wanted David's safety more than he wanted safety for himself. You can read about their situation in 1 Samuel 20. It's a great story.

Look at how Jonathan felt about David in verse 17: "And Jonathan had David reaffirm his oath out of love for him, because he loved him as he loved himself." That's true friendship.

True friendship is selfless. True friends want their friends to have the best. True friends think of others first. Do you treat your friends that way?

On the Chalkboard

Friends don't let friends get second best.

Sports Stat

In each of his first seven years in the NBA, Avery Johnson increased his scoring average each season. He began by averaging 1.6 points per game in 1988–89. By 1994–95 he was averaging 13.4 points a game.

- - - - - - - - - - - - - - - - - - - -*Instant Replay*

Who are my three top friends? What is something I know they want, and maybe I can help them achieve?

Sports Stuff

Avery Johnson is a great example of someone who didn't give up, and it paid off. He was a benchwarmer in high school until the end of his senior year. He wasn't offered a scholarship to college, but he ended up breaking two NCAA records for assists. And he wasn't drafted by any NBA teams; he was cut by the Spurs—twice. Yet he kept practicing and kept trying. Now he has an NBA title ring. If you need an example of someone who didn't quit even though things were tough, Avery Johnson is your man.

GAME PLAN

> This happened that we might not rely on
> ourselves but on God.
>
> 2 Corinthians 1:9

Play Book Assignment: Read 2 Corinthians 1:2–11

Double Trouble

Want to hear a sad story?

Matt Russell of the Detroit Lions was a rookie in 1998. During the very first preseason game, he blew out his knee. The injury meant he would have to have surgery and then spend the next ten months or so doing rehabilitation on the knee. Then he could begin to get ready for the 1999 season.

Which is exactly what Russell did.

So began the 1999 preseason games. In the first game, guess what? He blew out his other knee! That meant he had to go through the same painful routine for another year.

Talk about double trouble.

Let me guess. You've had trouble that seems just as bad to you as what happened to Matt. You've lost your homework, had your best friend move away, failed to make the soccer team, and found out that your cat is going to die. All in the same week. And then things got worse.

Why is it that really bad things happen to someone as nice as you? Where is God when you have more trouble than a kid should have? Is he not paying attention? Is he on vacation?

It might help to understand a couple of things about problems. First, just because you're a Christian doesn't mean you won't have any trouble. Look at what happened to the guy many think was the greatest Christian ever: Paul. He was thrown in jail, beaten, shipwrecked, jeered, and mocked. And he even asked God three times to take away a specific problem, but God didn't do it (2 Corinthians 12:7–10). Second, God has a reason for the trouble we go through. In 1 Peter, we're reminded that we suffer these trials so that God can be praised and honored.

Here's the most important thing to remember: our Christian life is not about us. It's easy to think that God is there to serve us. But it's the other way around. We're here to serve him, and if it takes trials for him to get the honor he deserves, then that's the way it should be.

On the Chalkboard

What we call trouble, God might be calling an opportunity.

-*Instant Replay*

What is my greatest problem right now? How can I make
sure God gets the glory as I struggle through this?

Sports Stuff

Some injuries in sports can't be avoided. Others can. For
instance, if you're into skateboarding or in-line skating, be
sure to wear a helmet, knee pads, wrist guards, and elbow
pads. It may not seem cool, but it's not especially "cool" to
have a concussion either. In sports like baseball, football, and
basketball, warming up properly and then stretching your
muscles may help prevent injuries. In baseball, using the
right technique for throwing will help you not to wreck your
arm. Take a little extra time to make sure you don't bring on
injuries that can be avoided.

The Lord disciplines those he loves.

Hebrews 12:6

Play Book Assignment: Read Hebrews 12:1–11

Stop Yelling at Me!

Coaches come in all shapes, sizes, and styles. But what most kids are interested in when they begin a new sport is this: "Is my coach going to yell at me?"

Some coaches think the best way to get their point across is to YELL AT YOU REALLY LOUD SO YOU DON'T MISS WHAT THEY ARE SAYING!!!!! Those coaches aren't too much fun.

Others might not be quite so loud, but they can throw some zingers your way that make your ears burn.

The next time you watch the NCAA men's and women's basketball tournaments, notice the coaches. There are the Bobby Knight–type coaches who look as if they're about to explode. There are the Pat Summitt–type coaches who are intense and serious but under control. Back in the 1970s, there was a coach who some say was the greatest coach of the twentieth century. His name was John Wooden. He would sit calmly on the bench with a rolled-up program in his hands. He never yelled or screamed. He simply talked to his players, guiding them quietly through their game plan. His method worked. His team, UCLA, won ten NCAA titles.

No matter what style your coach displays, there will come times when he or she will have to point out some things you're doing wrong. Your response will go a long way toward telling what kind of athlete you will be.

If you listen and learn, you'll get better. If you pout and refuse to learn, you'll never improve.

This old saying has helped a lot of young athletes: "The player who is never criticized is the one who should worry." In other words, if your coach never yells at you, it may be because he or she doesn't consider you a key part of the team. Coaches tend to spend the most time on players who will help the team.

Let's look at this idea in relation to your faith. God, like a coach, may find it necessary to discipline you. When he does, listen and learn. He knows what's ahead, and he knows just what you need.

On the Chalkboard

Learning from God takes listening to God.

Sports History Note

In twenty-nine years of coaching at the college level, John Wooden compiled a record of 664 wins and just 162 losses. He coached two seasons at Indiana State (1946–47 and 1947–48) and twenty-six years at UCLA (1948–1975).

------------------ -*Instant Replay*

In what ways have I ever felt that God was guiding me to change what I was doing? Did I listen?

Sports Stuff

Being criticized by a coach is never fun. However, you can help make the best of the situation. First, stop what you're doing and look your coach in the eye. Second, listen closely to what the coach says. Third, if you have to respond, don't do so in an argumentative way. Be respectful. Fourth, avoid trying to show the coach up after he or she has talked to you. Go out and try your best to correct your error.

For the eyes of the LORD range throughout the earth to strengthen those whose hearts are fully committed to him.

2 Chronicles 16:9

Play Book Assignment: Read Psalm 34:15–18

Tough Guy; Tough Talk

Chad Hennings is one tough guy. He's six feet six inches tall. weighs nearly 300 pounds, bench presses 530 pounds. And every week during the football season, he battles the baddest, strongest brutes in the NFL. Toe to toe. Helmet to helmet.

As an offensive lineman for the Dallas Cowboys, Chad has the job of protecting his quarterback and running backs against a bunch of people who want to pound them into the ground. Yes, Chad Hennings knows what it means to be tough.

So when he talks tough, you better listen. Especially when he talks tough about being a Christian. Hennings is a believer in Jesus Christ who strives to serve the Lord.

Here's what he says about toughness. "Being a Christian is tougher than being a non-Christian," he said in an article in *Sports Spectrum* magazine. "You have to work at it. Just because we are Christians doesn't mean we are not going to suffer pain. Life is hard. But we have to remember that when life is hard, God is there for us."

He's right, isn't he? Life can be hard sometimes.

Often, things at home can be really rough. Problems with parents. Or parents with problems.

Maybe you're struggling with tough stuff that happens outside your home. Perhaps someone you thought was your friend has suddenly turned on you and talked mean about you behind your back.

Or perhaps school life is very difficult for you. While other kids are writing down answers to their math homework as fast as they can, you struggle to get through the first problems on the page.

Tough times can come in sports too. You don't make the team. Or if you do, you hardly get to play.

One thing to remember is that you are not alone. Many, many kids go through similar problems. Even the ones who seem to have it all together are probably hiding something that's bothering them.

But the most important thing to do is to take a hint from big Number 95 of the Cowboys. "When life is hard, God is there." Chad knows. His son, Chase, struggled for a long time with a mysterious disease. No matter how tough Chad is, that was very difficult. Yet he says, "God is there."

You never have to go through your tough times by yourself. God is watching, and he is "attentive to [your] cry" (Psalm 34:15).

And you know what? God's tougher than any problem you'll ever face.

On the Chalkboard

There's nothing you're going through that God can't help you survive.

Chad Hennings's Note

Chad didn't play in his first NFL game until he was twenty-seven years old. Because he went to the Air Force Academy, he had a military commitment to fulfill before he could suit up for the Dallas Cowboys.

---------------------------*Instant Replay*

What is my toughest problem? Have I ever thought to talk to God about it and give it to him?

Sports Stuff

In order to make himself a better football player, Chad Hennings would spend a lot of time lifting weights. Could weight lifting help you? If you want to start, make sure you talk to someone who knows how to do it right. Lifting improperly could damage your muscles, or it might be the wrong kind of lifting for the sport you play.

> For just as the sufferings of Christ flow over into our lives, so also through Christ our comfort overflows.
>
> 2 Corinthians 1:5

Play Book Assignment: Read 1 Peter 2:19–23

Not Fair!

For a few years before becoming a writer, I was a high school basketball coach. When I get together with some of my old players, the conversation usually rolls around to a couple of bad things that happened to our team.

One was the time we had a two-point lead with four seconds left, and a player on the other team hit a three-quarter court shot at the buzzer to send the game into overtime (this was before three-point shots). We ended up losing the game. The other frequently mentioned event was when we were in the district semifinals, and one of our players missed a game-winning layup at the buzzer. We lost that game too.

We all can laugh now as we remember how much it hurt to lose those games and how unfair it seemed.

But those two losses don't compare with something else that happened when I coached.

One of my players died.

One day he was the happiest, friendliest, most energetic kid. The next day we were trying to cope with the word *cancer*. About a year after we first found out that Keith was sick, six of my basketball players were pallbearers at his funeral.

Losing games was bad, but losing Keith was devastating. That's when you start to say, "It's not fair!"

What can you do when life isn't fair? Give up?

Never.

You talk to Jesus. Above anyone who ever lived on earth, Jesus knows what "Not fair!" means. After all, he left the unbelievable home he had in heaven to live as a poor carpenter's son in Israel. Then, when he grew up as the first perfect human ever, he was captured like a common criminal. He was beaten and mocked. Even his innocence couldn't protect him from being crucified.

Jesus Christ can help us with life's unfairness because he understands. He went through it for us, and he wants us to tell him our troubles. He trusted God when he faced unfairness, and he wants us to trust him when we run into the same problem.

Life seem unfair? Tell Jesus.

On the Chalkboard

The world may not be fair, but Christ's sacrifice makes it good.

- - - - - - - - - - - - - - - - - - -*Instant Replay*

When I get down about something that I think
shouldn't have happened, would it help to read about
what Jesus went through for me?

Sports Stuff

Not all athletes who hear the word *cancer* from their doctor lose
their lives. Lance Armstrong, a cyclist, was diagnosed with
cancer. After treatment and recovery, he won the Tour de
France, the most grueling bicycle race in the world. It pays to
have a doctor look you over on a regular basis to make sure you
have a clean bill of health.

Saul replied, "... you are only a boy."

1 Samuel 17:33

Play Book Assignment: Read 1 Samuel 17:32–50

Too Small?

Brett Butler, Chad Curtis, and Avery Johnson all had a problem. They wanted to play sports, but they weren't big enough. People kept telling them to give it up—that they'd never make it, so they might as well stop trying.

There's probably something you'd like to do in life, but you're too small or too tall or too young or too something. When you feel that way, it's easy to give up on your dreams, isn't it?

Think of what would have happened if David had said he was too small to fight Goliath.

Or if God had let Moses refuse to lead the people of Israel because he wasn't a good speaker.

Or if Caleb had thought it was impossible to take the Promised Land because he was too old.

Everybody has something that isn't perfect about them. But do you think people ever get anywhere by worrying about what they can't do?

Let's put God in this situation (well, he's already in it, but you know what I mean). He has a little bit to do with the way you are. After all, he made you.

And he made you for a reason. Just the way you are.

God wants to use you just as you are. He wants to use the special characteristics he gave you.

Which brings us back to Brett, Chad, and Avery. Although they kept hearing that they were too small, they kept trying. They kept trusting that God would honor them for using the skills he had given them. That's why Brett Butler had a great career with the Cleveland Indians and Atlanta Braves, how Chad Curtis got to be a member of the 1998 and 1999 World Series Champion New York Yankees, and how Avery Johnson got a ring as a member of the 1999 NBA Champion San Antonio Spurs.

Too small? Not in God's eyes.

On the Chalkboard

God don't make no junk.

Speaking of Short

The shortest baseball player ever was twenty-six-year-old Eddie Gaedel. He was just three feet seven inches tall when he pinch-hit for the St. Louis Cardinals in a 1951 game against the Detroit Tigers. Wearing number 1/8, he walked on four pitches. It was his only major league at bat.

- - - - - - - - - - - - - - - - - - - -*Instant Replay*

What do I think my biggest problem is? How can God use me and my questionable characteristic?

Sports Stuff

To overcome a weak area, the best thing to do is to get better in some other area. If you want to be a basketball player, but you think you're too short, then become the best ball handler you can be. And never give up working on your shot. If you want to be in baseball, but you know you aren't very good, then begin now to prepare for something like broadcasting, sportswriting, or working in a team office. Spend time on your interests and what you do well, and stop worrying about what you can't do well.

> But you are a shield around me, O LORD; you bestow glory on me and lift up my head.
>
> Psalm 3:3

Play Book Assignment: Read Psalm 3

God Makes the Difference

Greg was crushed.

A fine athlete who loved baseball, eleven-year-old Greg was stunned to find out that his parents were getting a divorce. Nothing seemed as much fun anymore as he tried to cope with the fact that his parents would no longer be together.

About three years later, more bad news came. His knee began bothering him. Although he was a very good baseball player with a bright future, his doctor told him he couldn't play anymore.

Divorce. No baseball. Was there any hope?

Yes. Hope would soon come in the form of people who told his parents about Jesus Christ. One after the other, Allen and Sylvia McMichael trusted Jesus as their Savior. Soon, to everyone's amazement, they began seeing each other again and eventually got married. A second time. To each other.

Greg soon trusted Christ too. That redirected his life, which had started to spin out of control. He had begun sampling the party life, and it was wrecking the possibility of ever going anywhere in baseball, which, despite what his doctor told him, he was still playing.

It would make the story really good if the next thing that happened was that his knees healed completely and he never had another problem with them. Although that didn't happen, Greg did find ways to deal with having bad knees. He dealt with it so well that he became a major-league pitcher with the Atlanta Braves. He even pitched in the World Series.

How could all of this happen to Greg McMichael?

You'll notice that there were two kinds of problems in this story. One was created by people. That was the divorce of Greg's parents. The other problem happened to Greg even though he didn't do anything wrong.

The solution to both situations, though, involved God's work. First, through the Holy Spirit, Greg's folks were saved. Second, through his own salvation, Greg turned his life around. Instead of throwing it all away on sinful stuff, he became a success.

Some of the things that happen to you will be your fault; some won't. In either case, the answer is God. Don't run from God as Greg started to when things got hard. That's a mistake a lot of young people make. Instead, when things get tough, sit down and talk to God. Just do as the psalm writer did when he said, "To the Lord I cry aloud" (Psalm 3:4).

God knows all about what's going on in your life anyway. Why not talk to him about it? Then take the next step and ask him to help you make it. He may not take away all your problems, but he'll sure be with you as you struggle through life's difficult times.

Don't let bad things stop you. Let God make a difference in your life.

On the Chalkboard

No matter what the problem, God's care is the solution.

- - - - - - - - - - - - - - - - - - - -*Instant Replay*

Do I have a major problem right now that I'm trying to deal with? How can God make a difference?

Sports Stuff

Greg McMichael recorded saves in his first fifteen save opportunities with the Atlanta Braves in 1993, but he wasn't a pitcher with an overwhelming fastball. He got to the majors through being a smart pitcher. He learned how to be a pitcher, not a thrower. What can you do to overcome a lack of something in your game? The best thing you can do is to study the game and be the most intelligent player out there. Sometimes, knowing the game will get you further than pure talent.

Get Mark and bring him with you.

2 Timothy 4:11

Play Book Assignment: Read Acts 15:36–41

This Cut Hurts

Want to make a grown-up cry?

Find one who was cut from a sports team when he or she was younger, and then ask that person to tell you about it.

If you know much about Michael Jordan, you know that he was once cut from a basketball team. Actually what happened was that Michael tried out for the varsity team and was told he would have to play on junior varsity.

I know that can hurt, because it happened to my daughter one time. She was a high school sophomore who thought she had earned a shot at the varsity basketball team. When she was told she would have to spend one more year on JV, she was pretty upset. Tears and everything.

I know it can hurt, because when I was a senior in high school, I was cut from the varsity squad. After playing from seventh grade through my junior year, I was told, "See ya." From the time I was twelve, my deepest desire was to be on that varsity team and to play in front of my friends. But the coach had other plans. Ouch! That still hurts.

So, how do you handle things when they hurt like that? What do you do when you are really, really feeling rejected? When you have to look up to see the curb?

There's a Bible character who got cut from the team one time. His name is John Mark, and he was cut from Paul's missionary team.

In Acts 15, you can read about the powwow between Paul and his partner, Barnabas. They were talking about taking a trip to visit the Christians in some of the towns where they had preached earlier. Barnabas wanted to take John Mark with him, but Paul didn't. Paul said that John Mark had failed on an earlier mission, and Paul apparently didn't trust him.

Paul and Barnabas couldn't agree, so they split up. Barnabas took John Mark with him, and Paul went another direction.

That must have been embarrassing for John Mark. But you know what he did? He worked himself back into Paul's favor. In 2 Timothy 4:11, Paul said, "Get Mark and bring him with you, because he is helpful to me in my ministry."

Apparently, John Mark recovered from his disappointment and continued to work hard for God. Paul noticed it, and he let Mark rejoin the team.

We can learn a lot from Mark. His failure didn't stop him from doing great things for God.

On the Chalkboard

How you respond to rejection reveals how
well you'll rebound from it.

- - - - - - - - - - - - - - - - - - - -*Instant Replay*

How have I been rejected recently?
What can I do to follow John Mark's example?

Sports Stuff

Want to avoid being cut from the team? Know what coaches
are looking for. Of course, they're first looking for some athletic ability. But beyond that, everything else is something you
can do to improve your chances. Here are seven keys to
impressing the coach:

1. Have a great attitude.
2. Hustle all the time on the court or field.
3. Be a team player.
4. Listen closely to instructions and do exactly as you're
   told.
5. Learn the drills and perform them as designed.
6. Take the sport seriously.
7. Stay under control when things don't go your way.

G A M E P L A N

Live such good lives among the pagans
that, though they accuse you of doing
wrong, they may see your good deeds and
glorify God on the day he visits us.

1 Peter 2:12

Play Book Assignment: Read Hebrews 12:1–15

Making an Impression

They should call it the "embarrassment card."

In soccer, when you do something really bad, the ref runs over to you, pulls a red card out of his or her pocket, and shoves it in your face. When you see that dreaded red, you are one sunk soccer player.

In front of your team, the other team, and everybody else who's standing or sitting around the sidelines watching, you have just been kicked out of the game. No warning. No chance to do better next time. It's simply "See ya later."

You get one of those, and your ears will glow like a sunburn on a hot August day. You know you've done something really wrong, and you've just made a terrible impression on everybody there.

There's a team of professional soccer players who make it their goal to avoid getting any red cards. In fact, they don't even want yellow, which is a warning.

The team is the Charlotte Eagles of the United States Interregional Soccer League (USISL). This squad is made up of Christian players, and they're trying to be a witness to others of their faith in Jesus Christ.

Therefore, they don't want to make a bad impression. "Our goal is to go through the season without getting any yellow and red cards," the Eagles' general manager Tom Engstrom said. "We want to be an example that you can have the highest level of sportsmanship and compete."

That's a great goal for all of us. Even if we're not playing pro soccer. Even if we're just playing a little one-on-one in the driveway. Or even if we're playing Scrabble in the family room.

Making a good impression by staying under control goes far beyond how you act on the soccer field. It also should show up in all kinds of situations. When a friend says something bad about you at school, how do you respond? At church when you don't get the recognition you thought you deserved for some good work you did, what's your reaction? At home when your little brother takes one of your CDs, how angry do you get?

Day after day you'll face situations where people will be watching your actions to see if you are what you say you are. Would they red card you?

On the Chalkboard

What we do speaks so loudly, people sometimes can't hear what we say.

Speaking of Sportsmanship

The Charlotte Eagles won the Sportsmanship Award the first three years the USISL gave out the award.

- - - - - - - - - - - - - - - - - - - -*Instant Replay*

What are some things I know in my life are red-card things— stuff I know I shouldn't do because they make the wrong impression on people who need to know Jesus?

Sports Stuff

Want to avoid getting a red card? Learn what the officials are looking for. Here's what they can give you a red card for doing: (a) committing an act of violence or a serious foul, (b) using foul or abusive language, and/or (c) continuing to break the rules after a caution.

As the deer pants for streams of water, so my soul pants for you, O God.

Psalm 42:1

Play Book Assignment: Read John 7:37—39

Thirsty?

You've just spent the last hour practicing your ballhandling and your shooting. You're hot and sweaty. What's the first thing you do?

If you're like most athletes, you go for something to drink.

Watch any tennis match or any sports team. What do the players do when there's a time-out? They reach for the water bottle or the Gatorade or the Powerade.

That's smart. The body loses a lot of liquids when we exercise, and the best way to get them back into the system is by taking a nice long swig of something wet.

Well, not just anything. Some things are better for you when you are thirsty than others. Water is best. Sports drinks are great. But a cola is not so good at that time. In fact, that kind of drink doesn't help with the main problem. Instead of giving your body what it needs, a cola makes the problem worse because it dehydrates rather than restores liquids.

Did you know you can get spiritually thirsty too?

If it's been a few days since you've prayed or read the Bible or gone to church, you might be able to understand what that means. You don't really think about God much. You find it easy to think some thoughts you shouldn't think. You're thirsty.

In Psalm 42, you can see how David described being thirsty in that way. He said it's like a deer that can't wait to get to a stream and drink.

When that happens, instead of heading for the water bottle, head for Jesus. Listen to this invitation: "If anyone is thirsty, let him come to me and drink. Whoever believes in me, as the Scripture has said, streams of living water will flow from within him" (John 7:37–38).

Here are some of the things Jesus can give you when you turn to him: peace, joy, contentment, love, understanding, hope, and answers to your problems.

Talk to Jesus. It's the coolest drink you'll ever take.

On the Chalkboard

Jesus is the Well that will never run dry.

- - - - - - - - - - - - - - - - - -*Instant Replay*

What makes me the thirstiest when I get away from it? Missing Bible reading? Not praying? Not being in church?

Sports Stuff

What should you drink when you are playing sports?

That depends on how long you are training. If you're competing for longer than an hour, then sports drinks can be helpful. They give you an energy boost and can help the body absorb fluid faster than water can. If you're training or competing for less than an hour, just use water.

May our Lord Jesus Christ himself and God our Father, who loved us and by his grace gave us eternal encouragement and good hope, encourage your hearts and strengthen you in every good deed and word.

2 Thessalonians 2:16–17

Play Book Assignment: Read Luke 5:1–11

You Failed. So What?

Everybody has a failure story.

You know, when you missed the layup and your team lost the game by one point. Or you kicked a soccer ball into the wrong goal. Or you hit a golf ball ten feet. Off the tee. While your friends were watching.

Aaaauuugggggh! Don't you just hate that! Makes you want to make like a gopher and dig a big hole to hide in.

So what happens after you make a huge mistake? After you embarrass yourself so bad you just want to change your name and move to Greenland?

Professional golfer Barb Bunkowsky-Scherbak used to feel that way when she would play a bad round of golf. She would fall apart and not know how to handle failure.

Here's what she says about a bad day on the golf course. "Normally, I wouldn't be able to hang in there. I would beat myself up inside. But now I can go off a golf course and let it go. Now I've got a different attitude."

Barb used to get pretty upset with herself about hitting a golf ball the wrong direction (perhaps your mom or dad has had that problem), but then something happened to change the way she thought.

She found out that there was something tons more important than golf. A golfing friend of hers told her about Jesus Christ. When Barb found out about him, she says, "I finally realized I couldn't do it on my own anymore." She trusted Jesus Christ as her Savior.

And that changed her attitude toward a lot of things. Including making mistakes.

"Before, I'd feel so humiliated if I had missed an easy putt. I used to think everyone was talking about me. But now I have peace."

Nobody likes to make mistakes. They can be soooooo embarrassing!

But the best way to get over them is to realize that if we know Jesus Christ, he's the only Person we have to really be concerned about. And we know he loves us more than we can ever imagine. We aren't alone. When we blow it, Jesus will be right beside us, offering his peace.

Back in Peter's day, he failed big-time when he couldn't catch any fish. When Jesus found out about it, he helped Peter with his problem. Now, he won't always fill our nets with fish, so to speak, but he will always listen and provide his comfort and help.

You failed? Who hasn't? Turn it over to Jesus. Talk to him about it. See what he can do for you.

> ## On the Chalkboard
> The only way you can really fail is
> if you fail to trust Jesus.

Weird Golf Fact

The oldest golfer who ever "shot his age" (had the same number of strokes for eighteen holes as the golfer's age in years) was Arthur Thompson of Canada. At the age of 103, he shot a 103.

-Instant Replay

My biggest failure recently was when I _____

_____.

Have I talked to Jesus about it and given it to him?

Sports Stuff

We've talked about the spiritual side of making mistakes in sports, but what about the athletic side? What should you do when you make a mistake?

1. *Don't blame someone else.* Sure, there could have been a coach or another player involved, but it's up to you to admit your error.

2. *Review the mistake*. Sometimes you can see a mistake on a videotape that Dad or Grandpa made of your game. Although it's painful, look at it again to see what you did wrong.

3. *Ask advice*. Ask your coach or your mom or dad how you could have made the play right.

4. *Practice*. If you missed a putt, get out on the practice green and hit ten in a row of the same putt until you feel comfortable.

In this you greatly rejoice, though now for a little while you may have had to suffer grief in all kinds of trials.... [They] may result in praise.

1 Peter 1:6–7

Play Book Assignment: Read 1 Peter 1:3–9

A Mother's Death

Life isn't supposed to happen as it did for Hubert Davis when he was sixteen years old. It was all out of order. Your mother isn't supposed to die when you're still in high school. Mom is supposed to hang around long enough to watch you graduate from high school and go to college and get married and give her grandkids.

She's not supposed to get oral cancer and die when you're in the tenth grade.

So, when Ira Davis died as Hubert was just old enough to get his driver's license, Hubert was mad. Especially at God.

"I struggled with why he would take away such a person," says Hubert. "She was the last person I thought should have to leave this earth."

For the next five years, Hubert struggled with the loss of his mom. On the basketball court, no one knew that his heart was broken. In spite of his loss, he had made his way to the University of North Carolina, where he played well enough to earn a shot at the NBA.

His friends at college, though, knew Hubert was hurting. So they asked someone to talk to him. The man told Hubert how to have a personal relationship with Jesus. Within a year, Hubert had trusted Christ as his Savior.

Of course, this didn't get Hubert his mother back, and it didn't even help him answer the question that still bugs him: "Why did my mom die?" But it turned his anger for God into love, and it was, as he says, "the best thing that's ever happened to me."

Becoming a Christian doesn't solve all of your problems. It doesn't answer all your questions. But it does solve your biggest problem—being a sinner cut off from God. Hubert Davis, who went on to play for several teams in the NBA, is an example of God's love in action. God's love during tough times changes us from being bitter to being better.

There may be something going on in your life that you can't understand. You don't know why God doesn't just swoop in and make everything better.

That's not how God works. He doesn't just wave a magic wand and remove our problems. Yes, sometimes he will heal someone or fix a mess. But whether he does or doesn't, we know he works with us to make sure that our problems make us stronger.

God knows what he's doing. And he knows what he is doing with you.

On the Chalkboard

The worst thing that could happen when tough times come would be not growing closer to God.

Instant Replay

What is a problem I have to deal with but don't like? What could God be teaching me through this situation?

Sports Stuff

Hubert Davis was one of the best three-point shooters in the NBA for several years. In fact, it helped him stay in the league, because he was a specialist at hitting the three. What part of your favorite sport do you think you could specialize in?

If you play basketball, could you become the best free-throw shooter? If you play baseball, why not become the best bunter? In soccer, develop the best throw-in. Think about what part of your game you'd like to specialize in. Then set up a practice schedule that will help you accomplish it. The best way to get better is through repetition. Get help finding the best technique, and then practice it hundreds of times a day.

Dear friend, I pray that you may enjoy good health and that all may go well with you, even as your soul is getting along well.

3 John 2

Play Book Assignment: Read Psalm 119:97–104

Get in Shape

Give me five. Right now. Put the book down and give me five push-ups.

Done? How did you do?

Okay, now give me ten sit-ups. I'm serious.

How was that? Still breathing hard?

Studies show that young people (that's you) aren't in the physical condition they should be in. Of course you may be different, but according to people who study things like that, kids your age watch too much television, eat too much junk food, and get carted around too much to be in good shape. Ever thought of walking to school?

So I thought you'd like to test that theory. If you're really up to it, go outside and run around the block. (I'll wait.)

Welcome back. How do you feel? If the jogging has you huffing and puffing, you'll know the study was right.

You don't have to be out of shape, though. You can start today to get your body in good condition by exercising, eating right, getting enough sleep, and avoiding harmful stuff.

Now try this. Give me five blessings from God. Follow that up with ten things you're praying for. And run through what God's love means to you. Huffing and puffing? Are you out of shape spiritually?

If so, let me suggest some exercises that will help you get your spiritual muscles buff.

1. Set aside some time every day to talk with God.
2. Make a prayer list of things to talk to God about.
3. Write down why you love God and what you can do for him today.

I don't know if anyone has done any studies to find out why kids are out of shape spiritually. You don't need a study for that. You know if that's you.

So make a decision. Get in shape spiritually or be a spiritual weakling. Which will it be?

On the Chalkboard

If you don't exercise your faith, you'll have heart problems.

Sports History Note

Did you give me the 5 push-ups I asked for? Well, if you did, you're on your way to world-record status. You need just 37,345 more to tie Paddy Doyle's best-ever mark for push-ups. Doyle did 37,350 of them in one twenty-four-hour period in 1989. Ready? Down and up. Down and up. Down and up . . .

------------------ -*Instant Replay*

How would I judge my spiritual fitness?

A. I'm a blob
B. I'm an average Joe
C. I'm a world-class fitness nut

What can I do to improve?

Sports Stuff

If you're really into exercising, then you don't need this advice, but if not, here's someplace to start. Why not make it your goal to put together a simple program of exercise. Start with as many push-ups as you can comfortably do. Same with sit-ups. And running. For the push-ups and sit-ups, add one each day. (Five today, six tomorrow, seven the next day. Just think, in 102 years, you'll catch Paddy Doyle!) With running, walk/run a mile, adding more running each day until you can run the entire mile.

You know when I sit and when I rise; you perceive my thoughts from afar.

Psalm 139:2

Play Book Assignment: Read Jonah 2

Oops!

Just in case you didn't know, three hundred dollars is way too much money to spend on a week's worth of laundry. It would be cheaper to throw your dirty clothes away and buy new ones.

That's why professional tennis player Tara Snyder was pretty upset. She was in Tokyo, Japan, to play in a tournament. While staying in a hotel, she sent some clothes out to have them cleaned. You've heard of the expression "taken to the cleaners," haven't you? It means that someone tricked you and stole from you without your understanding that the person was ripping you off.

Well, Tara got taken to the cleaners. The laundry people sent her clothes back. They were clean, all right. And she was cleaned out. The clothing bill was for three hundred dollars.

"I didn't know what to do," Tara says, telling her story. "I prayed really hard and then went to see the manager of the hotel. I told him that I had no money to pay the laundry bill. The hotel took care of it." In other words, they paid Tara's bill.

"God was looking out for me!" Tara says.

Do you feel that God is looking out for you? It's easy to see how he can do that. In the Old Testament book of Psalms, in chapter 139, we're told that God knows when we sit and when we rise. He even knows our thoughts.

Because God knows so much about us, we know for sure that he is looking out for us.

Think about what happened with Jonah. He messed up a whole lot worse than Tara. She made an honest mistake, but Jonah did something wrong on purpose. But God was looking out for him anyway. After Jonah got tossed in the water, he would have drowned if God hadn't sent the big fish to give him a three-day ride in its belly.

God has his eye on you. He cares deeply for everything that happens to you, and he wants what's best for you.

That's got to make you feel really special!

On the Chalkboard

There's no place we can go where God is not there.

Traveling Tennis Players

Want to travel and see the world? Be a tennis player. In one recent year, professional women tennis players played in the US, Russia, New Zealand, Tasmania, Japan, France, Indonesia,

Germany, Italy, Wales, Spain, Scotland, England, the Czech
Republic, and Canada.

- - - - - - - - - - - - - - - - - - -*Instant Replay*

How did God take care of me this week?

Sports Stuff

Tennis is one of those sports you can play when you're young
and carry it over to when you are, well, as old as your parents,
and beyond. If you aren't already a tennis player, why not get
a racquet and start banging a few balls against a wall (not the
garage door). It's a great time to learn a great game.

We put no stumbling block in anyone's path.

2 Corinthians 6:3

Play Book Assignment: Read 2 Corinthians 6:3–10

What to Do with Pressure

"Hey, Mike! Let's skip practice today. It's too hot to play soccer. Let's ride over to McDonald's for a milk shake."

"We can't do that! We have a game tomorrow."

"Oh, come on, man. What's it going to hurt to miss one practice? We don't do anything the day before a game anyway."

Have you ever faced that kind of situation before? It's tough to make the right decision sometimes when someone your own age pressures you. In fact, pressure from a friend is probably the hardest to overcome.

You probably hate this term, but it's *peer pressure*, and it can make you do almost anything.

NHL hockey player Shane Doan faces all kinds of pressure as a pro on the ice. But he learned early in his life that the best way to handle pressure is to let it make him a better person. While talking about some of the decisions he has to face as a Christian in the rough National Hockey League, he says that something he learned as a kid helps him even now.

"Peer pressure has never really bothered me that much," he says. "It almost makes me stronger."

He learned that as a kid growing up in Canada. His parents had a Christian camp there, and they expected Shane to set an example for the other kids at camp. Not only did he have to withstand peer pressure; he had to have a higher standard than the other kids.

As an adult playing for the Phoenix Coyotes, he realized that you can't get away from peer pressure. In fact, he discovered that the pressure was even greater because he began playing in the NHL as a teenager. He had to make decisions about how he would respond to things the older players on his team might suggest.

Let's go back to the opening story. What's the big deal if you skip practice with the other kid? What does it hurt? Soccer's not that important, is it?

No, soccer isn't. But being trusted is. Here's how Shane says it. "I am scared of making mistakes, not just because I'm hurting myself, but others too. It's tough to make mistakes and then try to show God to people."

One of the best reasons to resist bad peer pressure is that giving in makes it very hard to witness to your friends. Why would they want to know God as you do if your life is no different from theirs?

On the Chalkboard

**Getting away with something may cause
a friend to stay away from God.**

Sports History Note

Players in the NHL regularly join the league before their twentieth birthday. But rarely are they discovered before they are teenagers. One player was, though. In 1960, some officials from the Boston Bruins went to see a game of youngsters. To their surprise, the best player on the ice was twelve years old. The officials discovered that the kid's name was Bobby Orr. Six years later, he signed with the Bruins and became one of the best players of all time.

- - - - - - - - - - - - - - - - - - -*Instant Replay*

**What are some peer-pressure decisions I have to
make? How can I make them in a way that enables
me to witness for Christ?**

Sports Stuff

One of the biggest controversies surrounding hockey and Christians is the fact that the sport is so rough. Some people wonder how a Christian can play a sport where hitting people with teeth-jarring checks is acceptable. Here's what Shane says: "I have no problem with being on the ice and being very physical. David had the heart of a warrior, and the Bible says he was a man after God's own heart. I'm very competitive. I like to play a rough-and-tumble game."

GAME PLAN

> But in your hearts set apart Christ as Lord. Always be prepared to give an answer to everyone who asks you to give the reason for the hope that you have.
>
> 1 Peter 3:15

Play Book Assignment: Read 2 Corinthians 5:14—20

Will They Listen?

"Nobody will listen to me. I'm just a kid."

If you have friends who aren't Christians, do you ever feel this way when you think about telling them about Jesus? It's okay, because most people your age feel like that from time to time.

It's not easy to talk to a friend about stuff like this when you're young.

But if it's something you might want to do, consider some advice from a former Major League Baseball player. His name is Sid Bream, and he used to play for the Atlanta Braves.

In 1992, he scored the most dramatic run of the entire season. It was the final game of the play-offs between the Braves and the Pirates. Winner would go to the World Series. Loser would go home. The score was tied in the bottom of the ninth. Bream was on second. A teammate screamed a single into the outfield, and Sid raced for home. The throw came in, he slid, and he was safe at home. The Braves won!

As important as that victory was, Bream considers his salvation a much more important victory. And he has the following advice for you if you want to witness to friends:

1. *Earn your friends' respect.* For a baseball player like Bream, that meant showing up, working hard, and helping the team.
2. *Talk to God.* You need God's help, guidance, and direction. "Prayer prepares your heart," Bream says.
3. *Know what you're talking about.* That's why you need to listen in church and read the Bible.
4. *Be aware.* "We are the light of Christ," Bream says. [You] need to be aware that you're God's witness.

This doesn't mean you have to be a miniature Billy Graham or something before you witness. But if you're serious about helping your friends discover Christ, these suggestions might help.

Will your friends listen to you? If they're your friends, they will. And if you're prepared, you may just help them become "safe at home"!

On the Chalkboard

When your friends are ready for the gospel,
be ready to share it with them.

Sports History Note

Sid Bream's team, the Atlanta Braves, went to the World Series five times during the 1990s and won it in 1995. This was after having the worst record in their division in 1989.

- - - - - - - - - - - - - - - - - -*Instant Replay*

**Which of my friends would I like to try to witness to?
How do I get ready to do that?**

Sports Stuff

The play at home plate on a ball from the outfield is one of the most exciting plays in baseball. It involves as many as ten people—the runner, the next batter who signals to the runner to slide or not, the third-base coach, the catcher, the out-fielder, one or two infielders, the pitcher who backs up the plate, and one or two umpires. And if there are runners on base, there could be as many as thirteen people in on the play!

GAME PLAN

Become blameless and pure, "children of God without fault in a warped and crooked generation." Then you will shine among them like stars in the sky.

Philippins 2:15

Play Book Assignment: Read Matthew 5:13—16

Why Play?

Why do you play sports? Is it because your parents want you to? Is it because someday you want to play in one of the BAs: the WNBA or the NBA? Are you thinking you might get a college scholarship? Do you play just for fun? Do you play because your friends play, and you want to be with them?

There's nothing wrong with any of those reasons. As long as you have fun and don't take things too seriously too early, what can it hurt?

I'd like to suggest another reason to play.

This one comes from Keri Phebus, a professional tennis player. Keri played college tennis at UCLA, and she was very good. She was even an NCAA national champion while playing for the Bruins.

Listen to what Keri says about playing tennis: "I pray before I go out on the court that I'll give all the glory to God and that I'll give my best for him."

Why does Keri play tennis? So she can glorify God.

Did you ever think of that as a reason for playing youth soccer or Little League baseball? Did you ever think that amateur volleyball is something you do so people will think about God?

It's possible.

If you play hard, people will want to know why.

If you play fair, people will want to know how you can do that.

If you have a good attitude, people will compliment you and wonder how you can be so cool.

Then all you have to do is point to your WWJD bracelet or simply say, "I want to please God."

Just like that, you've turned a game of soccer into a way to point to God.

If you're a sports fan at all, you probably know about the big star athletes who are really good witnesses for Jesus. David Robinson, Reggie White, people like that. But they aren't the only ones who can use sports to tell people about God.

You can too. In fact, that's what God wants you to do. In Matthew 5:13−16, you can read Jesus's words about being "the salt of the earth." That was Jesus's way of saying that you need to do everything in a way that will make people interested in what makes you special. When they want to know, you can tell them about God.

Why play? So you can point out how important God is to you.

On the Chalkboard

The best sport in the world shouldn't be the one you play; it should be the one you are.

- -*Instant Replay*

**Have I ever thought about the fact that when I play
sports or games, I'm a witness for Christ?
How can I remind myself to do that?**

Sports Stuff

Do you play tennis? If so, it's important to make sure your racket is the right size and weight, and that it has good strings. Consult a local tennis pro or someone else who can help you find the right size racket. As far as the strings go, you should have your racket restrung as often in a year as you play tennis in a week. If you play twice a week, get it restrung twice a year.

GAME PLAN

> The LORD gave and the LORD has taken
> away; may the name of the LORD be praised.
>
> Job 1:21

Play Book Assignment: Read Job 1:1–3,13–22

Control and the Slugger

Major League Baseball player Tim Salmon is big, strong, and really, really good. He can hit long home runs. He can play gracefully in the outfield. He's a leader on his team.

When you hear about someone like that, it's easy to imagine that he's some big macho guy who doesn't care about people and who treats a kid seeking an autograph as if he's a bad dream. Sounds kind of like some guy who goes around saying, "Nobody's going to tell *me* what to do."

Well, that may describe some big star baseball players, but it wouldn't describe Tim Salmon.

This big slugger isn't a control freak.

"The biggest thing I've learned," Salmon says, "is that I'm not in control. No matter how much I think I can control my life, it's not up to me."

Imagine a Major League Baseball player saying that!

"I need to take whatever situation the Lord has put me in and realize I'm there for a reason."

What kind of situation are you in right now that you don't quite understand?

Some problem at school with kids who aren't a good influence? A difficulty at home because not everyone is getting along?

Maybe you or somebody in your family has just found out about a serious illness.

That situation can teach you several things.

First, it can help you understand what Tim was saying. "We aren't in control. God is."

Second, it can help you believe that even when bad things happen, God has something good in mind for you (Romans 8:28).

Third, it can teach us to keep trusting God, no matter what happens.

Do you know anything about the Old Testament guy Job? Here was a man who was almost as rich as a Major League Baseball player, amd yet he lost everything. His money. His family. Everything.

Well, not everything. He kept one thing. Know what it was?

His faith in God.

Job was the greatest man in the East, but he found out that he was pretty puny compared with God.

The earlier in life you decide that, yes, God is in control, the better off you'll be.

Whether you're a slugging outfielder or the last person on the bench for your youth soccer team, it's all the same.

The best thing to do is to say to God, "Thanks for being in control."

On the Chalkboard

What we think is ours is God's.

Speaking of Control

Speaking of control (or lack of it), in 1938 Bob Feller walked 208 batters, the all-time record.

------------------*Instant Replay*

What part of my life am I having a hard time admitting belongs to God?

Sports Stuff

Control is very important in baseball, whether you're a pitcher or a batter. To develop control as a pitcher takes practice. One way to do that is to make a target you can pitch to over and over. For example, hang a tire from a tree limb and practice pitching through the hole in the tire. Or draw a strike zone on a wall (not the garage door or near a window) and pitch to that. For a batter, control comes from being prepared mentally. Train yourself to look for the spin of the ball (so you know how it will break) and to make a split-second decision about whether or not to swing at it.

> I have learned to be content whatever the circumstances. I know what it is to be in need, and I know what it is to have plenty. I have learned the secret of being content in any and every situation.
>
> Philippians 4:11–12

Play Book Assignment: Read Philippians 4:10–13

What's Wrong?

Everybody has something about them that isn't perfect.

Just look around at the kids in your class. Some kids have braces, which means somebody thought their teeth needed a little help heading in the right direction. Some have glasses, which means their eye doctors determined their eyes aren't quite right. Others . . . well, you know what the problems are.

What's wrong with you? What difficulty do you have that you wish you didn't have to deal with every day?

Here's something that might help. It's from Jean Driscoll, the woman who has won the Boston Marathon at least eight times in the wheelchair competition. She knows about having something wrong. Her legs don't work, so she gets around using her own set of wheels. Look at how she handles what some would consider a big hassle.

"I look at my disability the way somebody might look at their glasses. That's the way I envision my chair. Somebody who wears glasses, that person puts those on in the morning, and then they forget about them the rest of the day. They don't go through the day thinking, 'Oh, another day with nearsightedness.' As for me, the first thing I look for in the morning is my chair. Once I'm in it, I forget about it."

What a great attitude! Driscoll, who is a Christian, is a great example of living out the verse that says, "I have learned to be content whatever the circumstances" (Philippians 4:11).

Now there's a challenge! If you can have the same kind of attitude that Paul (the writer of Philippians) had, then you can be happy even when things aren't right.

To be honest, Jean Driscoll didn't wake up one day when she was ten years old with the great attitude she has now. When she was your age, she was really, really upset with God for allowing the problems she has.

Jean always had a hard time keeping up with her sister and brother because even before she lost the use of her legs, she didn't get around as well as they did. She had a spinal problem when she was born, and she was never able to use her legs in a complete way. By the time she was a teenager, she wondered why God was picking on her.

Later, though, Jean trusted Jesus Christ as her Savior, and she began to develop a really close relationship with him. That helped her trust him so much that today she can look at her disability this way.

What's wrong with you?

Turn it over to God. Then remember Jean and her wheelchair.

It'll help you see that life is good despite the fact that you're not perfect.

On the Chalkboard

The best state to live in is the state of contentment.

- - - - - - - - - - - - - - - - - - -*Instant Replay*

**What about myself makes me discontent?
How can I find a way to think about my problem in the way
Jean Driscoll thinks about her disability?**

Sports Stuff

Is there something you need to overcome to be a better player in your favorite sport? Use that problem to your advantage.

Let's say you're a baseball player, and you're afraid of the ball. Admit that you are, and then get in there and prove to yourself that it doesn't matter. Each time you stand in the batter's box and refuse to back off when the pitcher throws, you gain confidence. Soon, you'll be using that fear as a reason to get back in and stand your ground.

And the boy Samuel continued to grow in stature and in favor with the LORD and with men.

1 Samuel 2:26

Play Book Assignment: Read 1 Samuel 2:18–26

When Am I Grown Up?

How old are you?

Are you enjoying being that age? Are you looking forward to being a year older?

If you're like most kids your age, you're eager to be one year older or more.

Here's another question. Are you pretty grown up for your age? Most of the time, the answer is yes. No matter if someone is ten or twelve or fourteen, he or she thinks, "Yeah, I've got it together. I'm pretty mature."

That's why parents and kids sometimes have little battles over stuff like clothes and rules and friends. It's one side telling the other that there's still some growing up to do.

Now what about growing up spiritually? Most of the time, you're not in as much of a hurry to make that happen. Maybe you're a little like Trent Dilfer, NFL quarterback. Dilfer was really slow to grow up spiritually—and he's willing to admit it.

"I thought I was mature when I came into the NFL," he says. At that time he was about twenty years old, and he thought he had this faith thing all figured out. "But God really showed me a great bit of adversity to mold me into the person he wants me to be."

It's not just young people your age who need to grow up spiritually. Adults do too. But we can't do so until we see that we have a lot to learn. We can't learn the lessons we need to if we think we already know everything.

Samuel in the Old Testament must have been the kind of young man who, like Trent Dilfer, knew he needed to grow up. He must have listened very closely to Eli the priest because continued to grow up and be more mature, while Eli's sons didn't. They never did grow up, but Samuel became a very mature man of God.

Samuel is a great example of a person who learned how to follow God from someone older. Do you know anyone who could be like Eli to you? Someone you could learn from?

So, how old are you . . . spiritually?

On the Chalkboard

Growing up spiritually is much more important than growing up physically.

Speaking of Being Young

The youngest Major League Baseball player of all time was Joe Nuxhall, who pitched for the Cincinnati Reds when he was just fifteen years old. Nuxhall, who was from a town near Cincinnati, pitched in just one game in 1944.

- - - - - - - - - - - - - - - - - - -*Instant Replay*

How can I tell when I've been mature about something?

Sports Stuff

Sometimes when an athlete is really good, he or she ends up playing with kids much older. Like the freshman girl in high school who plays on the varsity basketball team. That usually happens either because the girl has grown up physically before others or because she worked really hard to get ahead of her classmates. Here's a concept that can help you if you want to get a head start on others your age. Think: Somewhere, someone my age is practicing. I won't let her work harder, practice longer, or improve more than I do. When I play against her, I will be ready.

GAME PLAN

In your anger do not sin.

Ephesians 4:26

Play Book Assignment: Read James 1:19–20

That Makes Me So Mad!!

Your brother sneaks into your room, takes your favorite CD, and uses it as a Frisbee. Your mom decides you need culture, so she takes you to the symphony the same day your friends are all going to the amusement park. Your dog eats your homework (hey, it happens). Your dad tells you that he doesn't think you should watch that particular movie all the kids are buzzing about. Or the report you just typed on the computer disappears into space somewhere when lightning strikes and a power surge zaps your computer.

Or let's say you just scored the winning goal in your soccer game, and the referee calls off the game because your best friend was offside. Or ... well, you know what to put next.

We're talking here about one of those situations that makes you so angry you can't think straight. It's when you stick your head in your pillow and yell, "That makes me so mad!"

Athletes go through those emotions too, you know. Of course you do. You've seen them get mad on TV!

NFL quarterback Trent Dilfer knows about anger. He has to fight his emotions as he tries to move his team downfield toward a touchdown. He can get angry with himself for making a bad play. He can get angry at a teammate for dropping a pass. He can get angry with an opposing lineman who sacks him and then lands on him (ever have a 325-pound guy sit on you?). Hey, he can even get angry at his coach for making a decision he doesn't like.

Here's what Dilfer says he does: "My prayer has been that the Holy Spirit would control my emotions on the football field. What I pray to the Lord is that I don't sin in my emotions. I don't want to sin in my anger and my frustration when things go bad. I want to be able to depend on Christ and his leadership in my life. I don't ever want my emotions to interfere with my obedience to the Lord."

Wow! Now there's a prayer idea worth cutting out and taping to your hockey stick! Dilfer is smart enough to know that if he tries to stop his emotions by himself, he'll just get as mad next time as he got last time.

He realizes he needs some major, major help. Only the kind of help God can give.

So the quarterback puts his situation in Jesus's hands and lets him take over.

That's a good pattern to follow the next time you start getting mad.

On the Chalkboard

When you get angry, you lose the key thing that can help you: control.

Speaking of Anger

Anger can make you do stupid things. One year John Wetteland, an all-star pitcher, got a little angry about something on the field, and he hauled off and kicked a watercooler. Do you think it made him feel better? Well, not when he broke his toe. He couldn't pitch for several weeks because of it. That's what anger can do for you.

— — — — — — — — — — — — — — — — -*Instant Replay*

Okay, what is it that makes me really, really mad? What would happen if I were to turn that problem over to God and let him be in control?

Sports Stuff

Anger on the field or court will get you nothing but trouble. Most of the time when athletes show anger, it's either because of something an opponent did or something the umpires or referees did. It makes sense when you're young to begin ignoring those two parts of the game. If you decide right now that you will never yell at an official or in any way show disrespect for an opponent, you'll be on the way toward eliminating anger.

G A M E   P L A N

It has always been my ambition to preach the gospel where Christ was not known.

Romans 15:20

Play Book Assignment: Read Romans 15:14—19

Are They All Ready?

When you have a ball game, you like everybody to be ready, don't you? You don't want players showing up without their uniforms or the right shoes. You don't want the refs showing up in suits and ties. You don't want the coach to drop by and say, "Oh, yeah. I forgot we had a game. Who are we playing?"

There's something else you want your teammates and friends to be ready for. You want them to be ready to face Jesus Christ. If they aren't, if something tragic happens to them, they could face an eternity of being separated from God. That's the worst thing that could ever happen to someone.

NFL quarterback Trent Dilfer thinks about this quite often. Besides wanting his teammates to be ready for their games, he wants them to be ready to face God.

"I pray for the salvation of the non-Christians on the team, and I pray that my teammates will see Jesus through me today—that they will see Jesus living in me. I just try to lead by example, and I pray that the Lord will reveal himself to those guys and that one day they'll be saved."

Think about your friends. Are they all ready to face Jesus? Do you know if they are or not?

If you want them to know about Jesus, there are some things you can do.

First, like Trent Dilfer, make sure you're a good example of what a Christian should be. If they see you do bad stuff like everybody else does, they won't think Jesus makes any difference.

Second, ask God to save your friends. Pray that they will trust Jesus too.

Third, look for something you can give them that might get them interested in Jesus. Maybe a really good CD with some Christian music. Or take them to some fun event your church has going on.

Jesus is your Friend and Savior. He died for you. Isn't that something you want to tell your friends about?

On the Chalkboard

The best thing you can do for a friend is tell him or her about your Best Friend.

Speaking of Preparation

One year, Lou Whitaker, a second baseman for the Detroit Tigers in the eighties and nineties, was unprepared for the

All-Star Game. For some reason, he showed up at the park for the game without his uniform. He had to borrow a uniform to play in the game.

- - - - - - - - - - - - - - - - - - -*Instant Replay*

Who is one friend I don't think is a Christian?
How can I get this friend's attention?

Sports Stuff

When you have a game, it's important to prepare properly. One thing you must do is prepare your body by eating right—even the day before the game. Talk to a coach about what the right foods are for the day before and the day of a game. Next, make sure you get enough sleep the night before the game. Another thing you have to do is prepare mentally. Think about what you're supposed to do in the game, and even guide yourself mentally through some situations. Then make sure you're prepared with the right equipment. Almost everyone who plays sports has a horror story about forgetting his or her shoes or jersey. Have a checklist to make sure you don't forget anything.

> All Scripture is God-breathed and is useful for teaching, rebuking, correcting and training in righteousness.
>
> 2 Timothy 3:16

Play Book Assignment: Read Ephesians 4:17–24

What's the Matter?

The Bible is a great book, but it doesn't tell us everything.

It tells us about Jesus Christ and how to become a Christian. It tells us how the world began, and it tells us God's Top Ten things he doesn't want us to do (the Ten Commandments).

But it doesn't tell us whether or not it's okay to get an eyebrow pierced. It doesn't tell us how much TV to watch. It doesn't tell us what kind of music we can listen to.

What it does give us are principles—standards we can use to help us decide whether we should or shouldn't do certain things.

Let's see how that works with one of those issues we don't have a specific verse for. There is no verse in the Bible that says,

"Thou shalt not be involved in pro wrestling." Now a lot of kids—even Christian kids—like to watch this stuff, and they think it's okay. But how do we know for sure?

Why don't we listen to someone who has been a pro wrestler as he looks for principles from the Bible. The former wrestler's name is Tully Blanchard, and he was a huge star in the eighties. He made a lot of money. Got really famous.

But then he quit. He trusted Jesus Christ as his Savior, and suddenly he began looking at the stuff that went on in the squared circle in a new way. Of pro wrestling, he says, "It has nothing to do with your performance. It deals strictly with violence. The Bible says, 'If a man would smite your cheek, turn the other.' Pro wrestling doesn't exhibit the traits of the Holy Spirit (love, joy, peace, longsuffering). So I cannot be in that business and be a Christian."

See what Tully did? He considered the situation. He compared it with biblical principles, and he made his decision. As he looked at what Jesus said about responding to someone who hits you, Tully saw that Jesus doesn't call us to hit back. What's even stranger, he said we should let the person hit us again.

Tully knows that this isn't the way the pro wrestling world is run. To obey Jesus's words, Tully quit the business.

Now start applying that plan to all the decisions you have to make. Take a biblical principle, apply it to the situation, and then do what God's Word says to do.

It may take a little work to dig out the principles, but it'll sure save you a ton of trouble and indecision when it's time to stand up for what God wants you to do.

Take it from Tully.

On the Chalkboard

It doesn't matter what color Bible you get, as long as it's read.

More on Tully

When Tully was into pro wrestling, he was part of a four-man group called the Four Horsemen. "I was arrogant, cocky, confident, and proud," says Blanchard. And he was very successful as he and his friends traveled around the country and appeared on TV. But his life was a mess. He got busted for drugs, and he was in serious trouble. When he trusted Jesus Christ as his Savior, though, his life changed, and he was suddenly happy and peaceful. And done with wrestling.

- - - - - - - - - - - - - - - - - - -*Instant Replay*

What do I use to judge whether something is right or wrong? Opinions of my friends, what I see on TV, or what God says?

Sports Stuff

Real wrestling and fake wrestling. A lot of people are involved in real wrestling in high school and college. In the real sport, the game is fair, it's judged carefully, it's run by a set of rules, and there is a clear winner. Fake wrestling is not a sport, and it brings before your eyes and ears a lot of things that are ungodly and immoral. Be careful to understand the truth behind fake wrestling.

The prayer of a righteous man is powerful and effective.

James 5:16

Play Book Assignment: Read Psalm 138:1–3

You Figure It Out

Here's a mystery. Read it and try to figure out what happened.

A college basketball coach by the name of Jane Albright was attending her team's spring banquet. It was at the University of Wisconsin, where Jane coaches, and her players were there to receive their awards for another successful season.

Jane was waiting for her turn to speak when she began to have a really, really bad headache. Not just one of those headaches that a little nap and a couple of Tylenol fixes. This was a major wanging honker of a headache.

It got so bad that Jane had to be rushed to the hospital. As she lay on the hospital bed, she began to hear people talking about doing brain surgery.

On her!

The doctors had discovered that she was bleeding in her brain, and they were going to go in there and fix it.

When she heard that, Jane began to pray. At the same time, word was spreading to everyone who knew her or knew about her: "Jane is in bad shape. Pray for her."

As Jane lay there in that hospital room, she felt absolutely terrible. She began to realize that she might die. Instead of giving a speech at a basketball banquet, she could soon be having speeches made about her at her funeral. While doctors whispered all around her, she made a decision. In her pain, she prayed and told God that if he wanted to take her, he could take her. (Of course, he knew that already.) She was a Christian, and she told God she was ready to die.

A feeling of peace swept over her.

Soon the doctors took some more tests to make sure they knew what to fix when they opened up Jane's skull. To their surprise, their tests revealed that everything was okay.

The doctors were puzzled. All that blood from the hemorrhage—it was gone. They didn't know what had happened.

That's the mystery.

What happened to Jane? A bunch of well-trained, intelligent, hardworking doctors couldn't figure out what happened to her. Why did she get better without surgery? How did she remain alive?

You know the answer, don't you?

Jane does. "I really felt the power of prayer," she says as she recalls that surprising situation.

Prayer is the most amazing thing you'll ever see. Why not make it a habit to talk to God during the day?

It's not really a mystery, is it?

On the Chalkboard

If you're not talking with God, you don't have a prayer.

Women's Basketball

Not too long ago, there was no NCAA tournament for women. Until 1982, women college athletes were in the Association for Intercollegiate Athletics for Women (AIAW). Since 1982, the University of Tennessee has been the school with the most NCAA titles.

- - - - - - - - - - - - - - - - - - -*Instant Replay*

When was the last time a prayer of mine was answered? What was it? If it's been a while, should I be praying more?

Sports Stuff

Girls' basketball is growing by leaps and bounds. For girls who want to improve, these are the keys: develop good ball-handling skills (dribbling and passing), be able to shoot (preferably a jump shot), and learn the ins and outs of the game by paying attention to the people who are really good. If you do those three things, and if you spend the needed hours practicing, you'll have a head start.

> A friend loves at all times, and a brother is born for adversity.
>
> Proverbs 17:17

Play Book Assignment: Read Ecclesiastes 4:10–12

Help from a Friend

Which team is the most famous in baseball? It's the one with the most World Series wins, the most history, the most tradition. The one on which the most famous baseball player ever played. The one with the most famous stadium.

Now imagine what it must be like to play for that team. To wear the famous pinstripes of the New York Yankees. The team of Babe Ruth, Lou Gehrig, Mickey Mantle, Joe DiMaggio.

Well, another player named Joe got traded to those same Yankees, and he was one unhappy guy. He didn't want to go. He didn't want to live in New York, he didn't want to play in Yankee Stadium, and he didn't want to leave the team that traded him.

144

Joe Girardi is a catcher who was traded from the Colorado Rockies to the Yankees. Here's what he said about it: "I was scared to death. I was angry. I didn't understand why God would take me to New York."

What does a guy do in a situation like that? What would you do? What do you do when you have to do something you don't want to do?

Here's what Joe did: he depended on his best friend.

In his case, his best friend was (still is) his wife, Kim.

"It was amazing what Kim did for me during my first year in New York," Joe says. "She let me know that God had me there for a reason."

Joe didn't believe her, but he listened to what she said.

Within a year, Joe Girardi was jumping all over the Yankee infield, celebrating a World Series win. And he couldn't have done it without his best friend, Kim.

How are you are at listening to good advice from friends?

Let's say a friend tries to encourage you. Do you shut him or her off? Or if a friend tries to give you some advice, do you say, "You're not my mother"?

Not a good idea.

Life is tough if you try to make it alone. That's why God gave you friends and put you in a family (yes, it's okay to take help from the people you eat breakfast with). Notice that today's Game Plan verse mentions both friends and siblings.

Don't try to make it alone (Ecclesiastes 4:9 – 10). Like Joe, be willing to listen to a friend who really cares.

On the Chalkboard

The first step in looking for help is to look for a friend.

Sports History Note

Joe Girardi played on the New York Yankees team that won three of the last four World Series played in the twentieth century. The Yankees won twenty-five of the ninety-five World Series played in the last century. (No World Series were played in 1900, 1901, 1902, 1904, 1994.)

- - - - - - - - - - - - - - - - - - -*Instant Replay*

Do I have one friend I can count on? Does this friend bring me closer to God or take me further?

Sports Stuff

Joe Girardi was especially valuable to his team because he was a true leader. As a catcher, he knew how to help his pitchers get better. One of the things he was good at was knowing what the scouting report said (the team had a record of how other batters hit, what pitch they had trouble with, and things like that). Whatever sport you play, those are two great characteristics: make your teammates better by encouraging them and helping them, and study your opponents to know what they do well and what their weaknesses are.

God, who is rich in mercy, made us alive with Christ even when we were dead in transgressions.

Ephesians 2:4–5

Play Book Assignment: Read Ephesians 2:1–5

The Most Exciting Thing

Look at this list:

- Three NBA championship rings
- Tens of millions of dollars
- Record for the most consecutive games ever played by an NBA player
- A published book about your life and your principles
- Your own foundation that helps kids

What would you think of the person who has all those accomplishments if he said that none of them is the most exciting thing that ever happened to him?

You'd probably think he's a pretty outstanding person. And you'd be right.

As hard as it is to believe, none of those achievements is the top event in A.C. Green's life.

The list tells about five of the things that happened to Green during his long and distinguished career in the NBA. While playing for the Los Angeles Lakers, he won the rings. Later, he also played for the Phoenix Suns and the Dallas Mavericks before rejoining the Lakers in 1999.

Yet A.C. claims that the most exciting thing that ever happened to him was something that took place when he was seventeen years old. And it had nothing to do with basketball.

The summer after A.C. graduated from high school, he and a bunch of friends went to a church service. While they were there, the preacher asked his listeners to come to the front of the church if they wanted to trust Jesus as their Savior. Surrounded by nine friends, A.C. felt that he should go forward, and he did. That day, he became a Christian.

"It was August 2, 1981. And it's the most exciting thing that has taken place in my life," A.C. says.

Think about that. If you're any kind of sports fan or player (if you weren't, you wouldn't be reading this book), then you probably have dreams of accomplishing just one little, tiny portion of what A.C. has done in sports. It's been a dream career for him, and it's easy to be jealous of him. It all looks so exciting.

But think about this. The many things we can't do that he did don't really matter. Yet we can be made alive spiritually by accepting Jesus as our Savior. He will bring us back from spiritual death! Now, that's exciting!

Are you sure that you have put your faith in Jesus Christ? Is that the most exciting thing in your life?

Learn from the NBA's Ironman what is life's highlight. And make sure you've done what A.C. did.

> ## On the Chalkboard
>
> The greatest trophy in life is salvation — the only thing you can take with you.

How Did He Do It?

One thing that can never be said about A.C. Green is that he is a quitter. One time, as he was nearing the record for most consecutive games played in NBA history, he got an elbow in the mouth and lost two teeth. After a visit to the dentist and the purchase of a mouth guard, he was back in the lineup the next night, keeping his streak alive.

- - - - - - - - - - - - - - - - - - - -*Instant Replay*

What's the most exciting thing that's ever happened to me?

Sports Stuff

Do you want to be the kind of player your team can depend on, whether you run cross-country, play tennis, or throw the shot on the track-and-field team? Keep these three guidelines in mind:

1. I won't let anyone practice harder than I do.

2. I won't quit or slow down unless I'm physically unable to compete.

3. I will do my best at all times, regardless of the score or the circumstances.

GAME PLAN

What good will it be for a man if he gains the whole world, yet forfeits his soul?

Matthew 16:26

Play Book Assignment: Read Matthew 19:16–22

Happy?

What's going to make you happy?

Think of all the things you sometimes talk about having. Stuff you talk to your friends about. Maybe clothes. A new phone in your room. A better computer so you can get email easier. A cat. Okay, maybe not a cat.

Sometimes you have a chance to get what you want—just by asking. Like at Christmas, when you ask for something like a new CD player, and *whamo!* you get one.

Sometimes the thing you think will make you happy is a person. Maybe there's a teacher you think you'd like to have—or maybe one you think you don't want. Or maybe there's a person you think would be a great friend.

But did you ever notice that sometimes when you get what you want, it doesn't make you any happier? It happens all the time with adults. They get that car they had their heart set on, and all it does is bring higher car payments and lots of worries about somebody stealing it or hitting it with a grocery cart.

For athletes, that something they think will make them happy is usually a championship. That's what they work so hard for. Brian Harper was a baseball player with the Minnesota Twins in the 1980s and 1990s. He used to think, "If I could just get that championship ring, then I'd be satisfied." But then he began to notice that a lot of guys in baseball said that—only to discover that winning the championship didn't make them any happier. "You win the World Series, and a few days after all the celebration, you're still the same, and all you have is a lot of good memories and a ring," says Harper. "That doesn't bring satisfaction."

You might say, "Well, sure. Brian Harper has to say that. He probably never won a World Series."

Wrong! Brian Harper earned a World Series ring while with the Twins.

Listen to what he says. "Without Christ it doesn't matter what you have. Compared to a relationship with Christ, winning a World Series is no comparison."

Look at the Game Plan verse for today. It says the same thing, but it goes even further. It's not talking just about winning the World Series; it's talking about winning the whole world. It says that it doesn't do any good to have it all if you don't have God.

On the Chalkboard

Don't look for things to bring you the happiness that only God can give.

World Series Fact

The most people ever to watch a World Series game in person was 92,706. The game between the Los Angeles Dodgers and the Chicago White Sox was held in the Memorial Coliseum in Los Angeles on October 6, 1959.

- - - - - - - - - - - - - - - - - - - -*Instant Replay*

What do I wish I had because I think it would make me happy? How can I tell the difference between something that I can enjoy and something that will bring me true happiness?

Sports Stuff

Whether you want to be a softball catcher or a baseball catcher, there are three types of throws you need to work on:

1. The full overhand throw
2. The snap throw
3. The sidearm flip

You'll use these throws in different situations as a catcher.

GAME PLAN

I know what it is to be in need, and I know what it is to have plenty.

Philippians 4:12

Play Book Assignment: Read Philippians 4:10–13

Want Some Money?

How much is a lot of money to you?

Suppose your mom says, "Here's ten dollars. Go to the store and get a loaf of bread. You can keep the change." The nine dollars or so you get back in change would be a lot of money.

Or your dad says, "Here's ten dollars. Go to the bike shop and buy yourself a new twenty-one-speed bike." Yikes! Then the ten bucks would be a dinky amount of cash.

If your parents showed you how much money they get paid for their jobs, you'd probably think that's a lot of money. But then if you compared their salary to, say, NBA basketball player Kevin Garnett, you'd stop wondering why your parents claim poverty once in a while. A few years ago, Garnett signed a contract for about $126 million. Your parents would probably have to work for three or four hundred years to earn that kind of money.

The point is, money is kind of a hard thing to figure out. It's dificult to say what is a lot of it. Instead of worrying about that, the important thing for you right now is to begin developing godly ways to think about money.

Former baseball player Brian Harper, who made a lot of money as a major leaguer after spending quite a few years sneaking by on nearly nothing as a minor leaguer, has some pretty good advice about money.

"The Bible says to be satisfied with what you have," Harper says. "I have been without, kind of like Paul said, and I have been with. I've been poor and I've been rich. The key is this: 'I can do all things through Christ who gives me strength' (Philippians 4:13). The key is to put your trust in God."

Harper continues. "There's a verse in 1 Timothy 6 that I go by. It goes something like this: 'Command those who are rich in this world not to be arrogant or to put their trust in money, but to trust God who gives you those things to enjoy and to be generous in giving to others.'"

From what Brian said about money, we can find at least three important rules to live by:

1. Our strength for everything, including thinking about money, comes from God.
2. If we have money, we shouldn't brag about it.
3. We should be generous with our money.

If you get five-dollars-a-week allowance, or if your parents are gazillionaires, those rules still apply. Think about that the next time you start thinking about money.

On the Chalkboard

Count your blessings and count your money. But count on God, don't count on money.

Money and Baseball

In one recent year, there were more than three hundred players in the major leagues who earned a million dollars or more to play the game. Now that's a lot of money!

- - - - - - - - - - - - - - - - - - - **Instant Replay**

Do I think I'd be happier if my parents made more money? What things do I think I need? What can God give me that money can't?

Sports Stuff

You might think it's impossible that you would ever make money as an athlete. After all, you'll never be as good as Venus Williams in tennis or Mia Hamm in soccer or Ken Griffey Jr. in baseball. But there are thousands and thousands of young people each year who earn college scholarships because of their sports skills. Maybe that could be a long-range goal for you—to someday be a college athlete. Talk it over with your parents and ask them if your family wants to be committed to giving you the opportunities you need. Are there some youth sports organizations like Amateur Athletic Union (AAU) that you should get involved in as you try to reach your goal? Are there camps you should attend? Dream big.

Those who are far from you will perish. . . .

But as for me, it is good to be near God.

Psalm 73:27–28

Play Book Assignment: Read Psalm 73:1–17

What Happens When You're Good?

Have you been pretty good recently?

Cleaned your room when you were asked?

Didn't watch that bad movie some of your friends wanted to see?

Went to church without even complaining?

Fed the dog?

Even had devotions?

Now, that's being good.

So what happened? Did being good mean you got all As in school? Did it mean you didn't make any mistakes in your soccer game? Did it mean your parents won the Publishers Clearing House grand prize? Did it mean your dad drove home a Miata convertible and said, "Hey, when you turn sixteen, it's yours"?

No, no, no, and no, right?

Life doesn't work that way, does it? Even if you're a Christian—and a pretty good one at that—God doesn't always give you immediate rewards for being good. Sure, he knows what you've done, and he promises to bless you for doing what he says, but he never said you would avoid all problems if you do the right thing.

Volleyball player Jan Harrer knows that's true. Jan, who played in the Women's Professional Volleyball Association during the 1980s, says, "I wondered why those players who may not be following the faith have such success. Lord, why would you give me a bad tournament?"

A guy who probably wasn't a very good volleyball player once wondered the same kind of thing. The guy's name was Asaph, and we don't know what he was good at other than being a song leader for one of King David's choirs.

Anyway, Asaph looked around like Jan Harrer did and wondered why other people—especially ungodly people—were doing well while he—a godly guy—wasn't.

Here's what Jan said was the answer: "It's just a matter of trusting God that in the end he will provide." That's a lot like what our friend Asaph said: "You hold me by my right hand. You guide me with your counsel, and afterward you will take me into glory" (Psalm 73:23–24).

Asaph discovered that if he depended on God, God would always take care of him, no matter how bad things looked.

Forget Jan and Asaph for a minute. Think about yourself. Are you willing to trust God all the time — even when you seem to be having a grotesquely awful day?

When you're good and things go bad?

If you're willing to do that, then you know for sure that you really, truly trust God.

On the Chalkboard

Trusting God doesn't make your life perfect, but it does put your life into the hands of Someone who is.

Volleyball at the Olympics

Here are the winners of the women's Olympic volleyball competition since it became an Olympic sport in 1964:

1964	Japan
1968	Soviet Union
1972	Soviet Union
1976	Japan
1980	Soviet Union
1984	China
1988	Soviet Union
1992	Cuba
1996	Cuba

- - - - - - - - - - - - - - - - - - -*Instant Replay*

Do I think God owes me anything because I'm good? Or am I good because God deserves that from me?

Sports Stuff

In volleyball, one of the most important skills to master is the setup. If you want to be good at setting up a teammate for a spike, you need to practice placing the ball between one and a half and two feet from the net, and at least five feet above the net. Arch the ball so that it drops directly into position for the spiker.

It is necessary to submit to the authorities.

Romans 13:5

Play Book Assignment: Read Romans 13:1–7

Those People in Charge

Do you ever think, "I can't wait till I grow up and I'm in charge"?

Because you're a kid, it probably looks to you like everybody's in charge but you. Everywhere you turn, there's somebody else telling you what to do.

Even when you play sports. All you want to do is have fun, but it's not that easy. There's the coach, who says who can play and what to play. There's the referee or umpire, who is never, ever wrong. You go home, and there's your big brother telling you what you did wrong. (Of course, he's not in charge; he just thinks he is.)

Well, I've got a little bad news. You'll never grow up and be in charge. At least not completely. Okay, unless you're the president, but remember, he's not a king. Even he has to answer to Congress.

No matter where you go in life, there will always be somebody over you.

So the best thing to do now is to get ready for that by learning to respect the people in authority. That's what the Bible says in Romans 13. And although Paul wasn't talking about coaches and referees, we can apply what he said to them.

Listen to what Rhonda Blades, a guard who graduated from Vanderbilt University and later played for the New York Liberty and the Detroit Shock in the WNBA, says about respecting authority:

1. *Be consistent.* When you show respect this way, the people in charge will treat you better.
2. *Set an example.* Whenever you get a chance, show how you think people should act toward those in authority.
3. *Pray.* When you pray for the people in charge, how can you be against them?
4. *Develop a strong spiritual foundation.* That way you'll base how you feel on God's instructions, not on the way the people in charge look at things.
5. *Be a light.* If you live so that the people in charge know you're a Christian, you'll respect them more easily.

It's funny. The people who don't like authority and think they are their own boss have more trouble with authority than people who don't. If you argue with your parents and don't respect their authority, guess what happens? You get less freedom. But if you respect them and what they say, they'll trust you and control you less.

We respect authority because God has designed life to be lived with someone in charge—first him and then people.

You can honor God by honoring the people who are in charge.

On the Chalkboard

When you respect those in authority, others will respect you.

Rhonda Makes History

Rhonda Blades made the first three-pointer in the history of the Women's National Basketball Association on June 21, 1997.

- - - - - - - - - - - - - - - - - - - -*Instant Replay*

Am I someone who respects the people in charge? How do I show that?

Sports Stuff

Hitting the three-point shot is one of the most exciting things to do in basketball. It takes three things to be a good three-point shooter. First, you have to have good technique. That means you have to have the right form when you shoot. Second, you have to have enough strength. You don't have to be muscle-bound, but you have to have strong forearms and wrists. Do a lot of wrist exercises and curls with light weights to develop this. Third, you have to have confidence, and that comes only through hours and hours of practice.

We are therefore Christ's ambassadors, as though God were making his appeal through us.

2 Corinthians 5:20

Play Book Assignment: Read 2 Corinthians 5:18—21

Know Any Atheists?

You aren't supposed to call people names. Especially a name like "fool."

But God did.

He said, "The fool says in his heart, 'There is no God'" (Psalm 14:1).

That's pretty harsh. But of course, it's God talking, and you could see why he'd say that.

Imagine your name is Jasmine, and your teacher looked at your name on her grade sheet and said, "There's no Jasmine. Jasmine doesn't exist." You'd probably think your teacher was a fool.

There are people, though, and probably some kids you know, who don't think God exists. So what do you do with them?

You care for them. You show them some love. You help them whenever you can.

That's what happened in Dana Lau's life.

Now, unless you're her cousin, you've probably never heard of Dana Lau. She played college basketball for Northern Illinois University in the midnineties. When she arrived on campus at NIU, she was an atheist. She simply didn't believe in God.

Little by little, though, the influence of some Christian teammates and a coach got her attention. She noticed that these people were different and that they cared.

When Dana started having problems, she turned to her Christian friends. It wasn't long before their love for Dana convinced her that God existed, and she became a Christian.

That's what we're supposed to do. That's what it means to be an ambassador for Christ (2 Corinthians 5:20). We're supposed to represent God to the people we know. By showing them what love is all about, we can show them what God is all about.

Know anybody who doesn't believe? Instead of treating that person like a bad person, do things for him or her. Be kind. Be a good example.

Before you know it, that person will be asking, "What's with you?" Then you can tell him or her about God.

On the Chalkboard

Some people will never look for God if they don't see him in you.

Women's College Basketball

Since the NCAA started running women's basketball (the same group that does the men) in 1982, here are the all-time leaders in key statistics. Will you ever break one of these records?

1. Scoring: 33.6 points per game, Patricia Hoskins, Mississippi Valley, 1989
2. Rebounding: 18.5 rebounds per game, Rosina Pearson, Beth-Cookman, 1985
3. Most points in one game: 60 points, Cindy Brown, Long Beach State, 1987

- - - - - - - - - - - - - - - - - - - -*Instant Replay*

Do I know someone who doesn't believe in Jesus Christ? What can I do to show enough love to convince that person that he or she should do what I've done and trust Christ?

Sports Stuff

Dana Lau's strong point as a college basketball player was defense. If you want to be the best defender you can be, you need to understand some basic principles:

1. *Develop good footwork.* You have to be able to move side to side really fast, for instance.
2. *Learn to read the passes of the other team.* It's much better to steal passes than to try to steal the ball when someone is dribbling.

3. *Understand proper positioning.* For instance, if your opponent is one pass away from the ball, you need to be in denial position, ready to knock down the oncoming pass.

4. *Always be ready to box out when a shot is taken.* Never let your opponent get between you and the basket.

I call on the LORD in my distress, and he answers me.

Psalm 120:1

Play Book Assignment: Read 1 Peter 1:6—7

Don't Hit the Ref!

Rule number one in dealing with sport referees: don't hit them.

That's pretty easy. Simply don't hit the ref.

But that's what Tara Snyder did. She didn't mean to. She's not a hothead. She's not a troublemaker.

Yet, *bam!*

Here's what happened. Tara was playing tennis in a tournament in England. She won the first set 7—6 and lost the second one 4—6. In the third set, she was behind 0—1 (if she loses the third set, she's out). Then it started raining. Tara asked for the officials to stop the match, but they didn't, and she lost the second game. So, now she's down 0—2.

That's when the umpired decided to stop play.

Tara was upset because she was down 0−2, making it really hard to come back. She turned to throw her racket toward her bag, which was on the sidelines. She figured they were done playing, so what would it hurt?

Well, it hurt the sideline official it hit, although not much. Because Tara's hand was wet, the racket slipped when she threw it, and it nailed the guy in the shoulder. It didn't do any damage, really—just a glancing blow.

But Tara was in deep trouble now. The tournament officials decided to disqualify her from the tournament, and her name was blasted all over newspapers with the headline "Snyder Hits Official!"

Embarrassed, Snyder sought assistance. "I really needed God's help to get through it. I prayed and asked him to show me what to do."

She believed that he wanted her to keep going and play in the next tournament, despite feeling that she would rather go home and forget about it.

"I've always believed that things happen for a reason and that God works everything out. When we're knocked down," she says, "he can give us strength to get right back up. He's made me stronger through the whole ordeal."

Have you done something recently that you wish you hadn't? Feeling embarrassed about it? Maybe a bit down? Do what Tara did. Turn it over to God. Pray to him honestly and tell him how you feel. Trust him that he really can take care of you even when you blow it. Then watch as he gives you the strength to get back up and get going again.

There is nothing better you can do when you face trouble than to call on God. He'll forgive you and comfort you.

On the Chalkboard
Give your troubles to God and turn trials into triumphs.

Where Did We Get Tennis?

Most people who study tennis think it came from an eleventh-century game played in France. However, the game wasn't well known until the 1800s when courts began to be constructed in England. The first tennis club was begun in England in 1872.

----------------------- -*Instant Replay*

**What trouble have I gotten myself into?
Have I been willing to talk it over with God?**

Sports Stuff

Tennis is a sport in which good conduct is expected. There are several ways this can happen. First, as you warm up before a match, you try to hit the ball so that the other person can return it. This isn't the time to hit winners or make your opponent run. Second, you should be fair in calling balls in or out, since it is your responsibility to do so when the ball is on your side of the net. Third, you should never distract another player while the ball is in play. This includes yelling, applauding, or in any other way being disruptive. Tennis is a sport where the Golden Rule applies (Matthew 7:12).

GAME PLAN

Many are the plans in a man's heart, but it is the LORD's purpose that prevails.

Proverbs 19:21

Play Book Assignment: Read 2 Corinthians 1:15–17

Daily Checklist

Lots of people in sports keep a daily checklist.

Watch your coach next time you have practice. He or she will probably have a sheet of paper with a list of stuff to be accomplished at practice. Your coach will mentally check them off as practice progresses.

Athletes often have a mental list of things they do before a game. From the time they leave home until the time they step onto the playing surface, they have things mapped out.

Sometimes athletes have some rather odd things on their daily checklist. Baseball player Wade Boggs' list always included eating a chicken dinner before the game. Basketball player Mark Jackson's list always includes taking off his wedding ring and tying it onto the laces of his basketball shoes.

Checklists can be very helpful in your spiritual life too. Perhaps it would be a good idea to have a mental list of what you want to make sure happens each day as you try to live for God. To help you, here are four things professional tennis player Tara Snyder says help her each day.

1. *Stay focused*. Don't get sidetracked; keep your mind on what is important.
2. *Surround yourself with positive spiritual people.*
3. *Ask God*. Talk to God throughout the day, and he will give you guidance.
4. *Put God first*. Put him before sports, before everything.

In Proverbs we can see that God is in ultimate control, even when we set up our plans. No matter what our plans might be, if they aren't plans that God would approve, they won't succeed.

Notice also that the apostle Paul made plans before he decided about his visits to Macedonia. He thought ahead of time about what he was going to do.

Why not try putting together your own checklist? What four essential things do you think you need to do each day to build up your relationship with God and be the kind of person he wants you to be?

Then pray for God to guide you in what he wants you to do each day.

On the Chalkboard

No plan is a success unless God gives it his approval.

Sp ing of Lists

In 1999,   or League Baseball put together a list of the top
baseball pl. rs of the twentieth century.

Outfielders: Babe Ruth, Hank Aaron, Ted Williams,
Willie Mays, Pete Rose, Ken Griffey Jr., Rogers
Hornsby

Third base: Mike Schmidt, Brooks Robinson

Shortstop: Ernie Banks, Cal Ripken Jr.

Second base: Honus Wagner

First base: Mark McGwire

Catchers: Johnny Bench, Yogi Berra

Pitchers: Bob Gibson, Sandy Koufax, Roger Clemens,
Nolan Ryan, Walter Johnson, Cy Young, Christy
Matthewson

- - - - - - - - - - - - - - - - - - -**Instant Replay**

**If I do make plans, how do I know they are the
things God wants me to do?**

Sports Stuff

Make a list of goals for the sport you most want to improve in.
Identify one goal for each of these areas:

1. Improving my skills
2. Improving my knowledge
3. Improving my conditioning
4. Improving my leadership

But when God ... called me by his grace ...
I went immediately into Arabia.

Galatians 1:15, 17

Play Book Assignment: Read Acts 9:1–10, 17–19

Late Bloomers

It's not easy being a late bloomer.

I ought to know. I was one.

Although I'm six feet tall now, I was "the short kid" for a long, long time while growing up.

It was a real problem when I turned thirteen and had to switch from the Little League field—where I was crushing Little League pitching—to the major-league-size field. Batting champ at age twelve (Really! Wanna see the trophy?). Batting chump at age thirteen.

When baseball turned on me, I switched to loving basketball more than anything. But that just caused more problems. I had to struggle through two junior high years as the shortest kid on the team. It wasn't until I grew about eight inches between my freshman and sophomore years that I could compete on the high school level without feeling like the elementary kid who wasn't supposed to be there.

You know some other late bloomers?

David Robinson of the San Antonio Spurs is one. The Admiral stands about seven foot one now, but when he enrolled at the Naval Academy, he was six foot four. That's tall, but it wouldn't make him the starting center on the US Olympic team or a Twin Tower in San Antonio. He grew seven inches after he started college! That's blooming late.

And Jon Kitna, who became the Seattle Seahawks' starting quarterback in 1999. When he was fourteen, he was five foot two. A year later, he was six foot two and suddenly big enough to be a quarterback.

This kind of information can help you two ways. First, if you are struggling with some kind of late-blooming problem, it'll help you have patience. Hang in there; you'll grow to maturity eventually. You might not be as tall as you'd like to be—not many people are—but you'll be big enough.

Second, you can look at this spiritually too. Unlike what happens to your body, you can do something about being a late bloomer spiritually. You can do stuff that will help you grow up in your relationship with God. But don't wait too long. The problem with allowing too much time to go by without growing up spiritually is that in the meantime, you can make some pretty lousy decisions.

You might say the apostle Paul was a late bloomer spiritually. And, boy, did he make some crummy decisions before he matured spiritually. Before he became a Christian, he did everything he could to hurt Christians. He even held Stephen's coat while others stoned him to death (Acts 8:1).

After Paul trusted Christ, he still had a lot of growing up to do. He went away to the desert (Arabia; see Galatians 1:17) for a long time to learn about God before he was ready to be a leader.

Is it time to begin growing up spiritually? You don't want to wait too long to be the kind of person God wants you to grow up to be.

On the Chalkboard

Just because you are God's child and have childlike faith doesn't mean you have to act like a little kid.

Really, Really Late

In 1999, a former high school teacher who was in his late thirties made it to the major leagues. He had given up on baseball in his twenties, had become a teacher, but then he discovered that he could still pitch. So he went to the minors and worked his way to the majors. Wow!

- - - - - - - - - - - - - - - - - - -Instant Replay

**How mature or grown up am I spiritually?
Am I a baby, an elementary student, a high school student, or an adult spiritually?**

Sports Stuff

You might notice that you and your friends grow up at drastically different rates. Some grow up so fast that in the seventh grade, they are the biggest and strongest, and they seem to have the advantage in sports. But be patient, it mostly evens out eventually. While you're waiting to grow, do these things: Practice your skills and perfect them. Study the game so you know the ins and outs of it. Then, when your body catches up, you'll be ready.

GAME PLAN

> Let us throw off everything that hinders
> and the sin that so easily entangles [us].
>
> Hebrews 12:1

Play Book Assignment: Read Hebrews 12:1–6

Running Free

It was a cold, windy, miserable, rainy October day. A great day for a nice game of indoor anything. It was a rush-to-your-car kind of day. Only statues and penguins should have been outside.

But it was also the day of a scheduled high school cross-country meet. As the parents and the runners scurried around before the race, trying to pretend they were staying warm, one dad went up to his son and said, "Why don't you wear a sweatshirt under your tank top?"

The dad was thinking about comfort. The son was thinking about running fast.

"No. That'll slow me down," the son replied. "I'll be okay."

So the high schooler braved the cold in order to improve his time. And by the time he was finished, he wasn't cold anyway.

He crossed the finish line faster than he would have if he had been slowed down by too much clothing.

Whether you run on a cross-country team or not, you are in a race. And the best way to run that race is by taking off everything that might slow you down.

That's what the person who wrote the book of Hebrews said. He told us to toss off anything that slows us in our race for the Lord (Hebrews 12:1). For instance, if you have been doing something recently that you know is keeping you from God, "throw it away." Or if music or spending too much time on the Internet is keeping you from reading the Bible, throw it away (well, not literally—but put it aside).

What is the goal of a Christian? To be as close to God as possible. To reach that goal, sometimes we have to be a little uncomfortable.

The cross-country runner was pretty cold when he started the race, but he was rewarded by running better and even by not being too hot as he ran. By chucking his shirt, he ran better.

You will run your Christian race better if you don't have too much stuff slowing you down.

On the Chalkboard

You can't run God's race well if you have a backpack of extra stuff to carry around.

Speaking of Running

One person who must have really thrown off the extra weight when he ran was Edgard Campos Barreto of Naples, Florida. In 1987, he ran sixty-four marathons (twenty-six miles, 385 yards).

What's slowing me down? How do I get rid of it?

Sports Stuff

If you want to be a good long-distance runner, you need to build up a base of miles run. Each week, you need to set a goal of miles you want to run and then plan your week accordingly. The most important piece of equipment is the pair of shoes you wear. Make sure you get shoes designed for running (not basketball shoes) and that you get them fitted by a professional.

I have become all things to all men so that
by all possible means I might save some.

1 Corinthians 9:22

Play Book Assignment: Read 1 Corinthians 9:19–23

Hoops Roots

Do you know a lot about basketball? Players' names? Teams? Stats? Even some strategy?

That's good. But do you know anything about the game's history? Yes, history.

Before you stop reading because this isn't history class, let me tell you something about basketball that might really surprise you.

The sport was invented as a way to get the gospel of Jesus Christ to new people.

Yes, according to sports historian Dr. Tony Ladd of Wheaton College in Illinois, the inventor of basketball, Dr. James Naismith, wanted the game to be used in missions work. Look at what

Dr. Ladd said of Naismith: "Perhaps he could reach people with a new game. As a committed Christian, he wanted to invent a game that would provide a means for him and others to lead other young men to a personal relationship with Christ." That game was basketball.

Imagine that!

And think of this: the NBA. Michael Jordan's skills. Your high school's team. Your basket in the driveway. These all exist because one man was looking for a way to spread the gospel.

Of course, it didn't turn out exactly as Dr. Naismith had planned, but there are still plenty of people who used basketball as a way to reach people and tell them about Jesus.

But there's something else we can learn. This can help us see that everything can be used for God.

If a sport like basketball can be invented as a way to help people know about God, then think about how some other things you have or do can be used that way. The apostle Paul set the example when he talked about doing whatever it takes to reach people for Jesus (1 Cor. 9:22).

For instance, think about how your paper route can be a way to show God to people. By practicing honesty and reliability, you'll be a testimony.

Or what about your ability to play a musical instrument? That trumpet or drum can be dedicated to God.

Or your interest in animals. Could you find a way to use that as an encouragement to others who like them too?

If basketball can be used for Jesus, there shouldn't be anything stopping us from using our interests for him.

On the Chalkboard

The point of everything you do should be to point everyone to Jesus.

Basketball Begins

The first basketball game was played in late 1891. Here are some of the rules when the game first began: There were nine players on a team. A player could not run with the ball. He had to throw it after catching it. If a team made three straight fouls, the other team got a point. A goal was scored when someone would either throw or bat the ball into the goal. If the ball went out of bounds, it belonged to the first person touching it. Somehow, this game caught on.

- - - - - - - - - - - - - - - - - - -*Instant Replay*

What can I use for God that I've never thought of using before?

Sports Stuff

Basketball has changed greatly since it began in the nineteenth century. For most of the game's history, though, three things have been important if you want to be any good: ballhandling skills, shooting skills, and defense. Good ballhandling skills can be developed through drills and repetition. Develop a set of ballhandling drills that you go through every day (figure-eight dribbling, speed passing against a wall, circling the ball around your back continuously). Your goal is to make handling the ball second nature—something you don't have to think about.

> As for those who seemed to be important—
> whatever they were makes no difference to
> me; God does not judge by external appearance.
>
> Galatians 2:6

Play Book Assignment: Read 1 Timothy 2:1–6

The $126,000,000 Man

Back in the late 1990s, the Minnesota Timberwolves of the NBA signed Kevin Garnett to a contract that promised to pay him $126 million.

Do you know how much that is? For one thing, if you had that much money, you could spend a thousand dollars a day, and you wouldn't run out of cash for 345 years. You could buy 2,500 Corvettes, loaded. If you gave 10 percent to your church, the board would have more than $12 million to do some good things with (maybe they'd build a gym).

But did you know that Kevin Garnett isn't worth any more than you are? Even with his $126 million, you and Kevin have the exact same value.

The value of a person isn't based on how much money he or she has, but on how much God cherishes that person. And when you think about it, you'll realize that you and Kevin share this: you are both so valuable to God that he was willing to sacrifice his only Son, Jesus, for you.

Rich people, poor people, or in-between people. None of that makes a person more valuable than another. Jesus Christ "gave himself as a ransom [a payment] for all men" (1 Timothy 2:6). He died for all people, no matter their status. Everyone is the same in his eyes.

So, what does that mean to you?

Do you ever have times when you're sitting in your bedroom wondering about life? Do you ever think that you make too many mistakes to be worth much to anybody? Or that you can't really do all the neat stuff your older brother does? Or that everybody seems to be on your case all the time? Or that you're too ugly or have teeth that are too big or have really bad hair?

When you begin to feel that way, it's easy to think you're not worth much. But remember this: when Jesus died on the cross, he was saying that you were worth dying for. Jesus would have died for you if you were the only person on earth.

God was willing to exchange his Son for you. Whoa! That shows how much value he places on you.

So whether you make $126 million playing basketball or $8.98 a week on a paper route, you are special to God. Don't let anyone tell you different.

On the Chalkboard

Your value isn't based on how much somebody pays you but on how much God paid for you.

He Broke the Bank

No basketball player will probably ever make as much money as Kevin Garnett made. Not long after his contract was signed, the NBA went into a lockout. This meant that the owners wouldn't let the players play. During the lockout, the owners and the players made some agreements about future salaries. In those agreements, it was decided that there was a limit to how much a player could make. And Garnett's $126 million is above that limit.

- - - - - - - - - - - - - - - - - - -*Instant Replay*

What makes me sometimes think I'm not worth much? How does thinking about what God did for me help me not to get down on myself?

Sports Stuff

Who is my favorite sports figure? Does how much he makes help me decide whether I value him or not? What makes an athlete important to me? Have I ever thought about setting up some guidelines for the kind of person I want to follow?

GAME PLAN

> Have I not commanded you? Be strong and courageous. Do not be terrified; do not be discouraged, for the LORD your God will be with you wherever you go.
>
> Joshua 1:9

Play Book Assignment: Read Joshua 1:1—9

A.C. Fights the Crowd

A.C. Green was sweating.

There he was, sitting in the middle of all his friends, and he had to get out.

The preacher was giving an invitation, and A.C. knew he had to go to the front of the church. Yet none of his buddies were budging. He would have to crawl over them to get out to the aisle.

But what would his friends say? They had all sat through the same sermon. They had all heard the pastor ask them if they wanted to trust Jesus Christ as Savior. They had all listened as he told them it was a matter of spiritual life and death. But they weren't going anywhere.

Finally, A.C. took a deep breath and told his friends, "Excuse me, but I'm going down front."

That day, A.C. Green, who now holds the NBA record for playing in the most consecutive games (well over one thousand), trusted Jesus. He became a Christian. "On that day, August 2, 1981, I really got born again," A.C. says.

Ever since, A.C. has been resisting the temptation to give in. All the way through his long career in the NBA (he won NBA championship rings with the Lakers), Green fought the crowd in regard to something that will be more and more important to you as the years go by.

Everywhere around him he heard people say it's okay to have sexual relations with someone without being married, but A.C. refused to agree with that thinking. Throughout his NBA career, he spread the message that it's right and godly to live a pure life.

One thing you can say about A.C. is that he sticks to what he thinks is right, no matter what anybody says. He did that when he got saved, he did that by continuing to play in more than one thousand straight NBA games, and he did that by speaking out about sexual purity in an impure world.

Think about what you're willing to stand for. Anything? Everything? Nothing? Are you willing to fight the crowd? When people want you to do something that you know is wrong, are you willing to stand up to them, sweat a little, and trust that God knows what he's talking about in the Bible?

A.C. Green is a lot like Joshua. Do you suppose that when God told Joshua that he was going to be taking over for Moses, he sweat a little? You will too when you take a stand.

But if you trust God's Word, take courage, and depend on God's presence, you can stand up for anything (Joshua 1:8–9).

On the Chalkboard

Unless you stand up for Jesus in everything, you might fall for anything.

Speaking of Endurance

Another Ironman in sports is Cal Ripken Jr., who played in the most consecutive Major League Baseball games—2,632. But before he made it to the majors, he played in the longest baseball game ever. In 1981, he was playing for the Rochester Red Wings in a minor-league game. The contest went thirty-three innings before the Pawtucket Red Sox won 3–2.

- - - - - - - - - - - - - - - - - - -*Instant Replay*

**What temptation threatens me the most?
What can I do to make sure I stay strong?**

Sports Stuff

In order to be there when your team needs you, you have to take care of your body. Here are some key ways to make sure you can be as dependable as A.C. Green (well, almost as dependable):

1. *Get plenty of rest.*
2. *Avoid things that will hurt your body* (junk food, for instance).
3. *Wash your hands regularly.* It sounds silly, but this is the best way to avoid getting colds from others.
4. *Stay in shape.* Couch potatoes are spuds that are duds.

A wise man's heart guides his mouth, and his lips promote instruction.

Proverbs 16:23

Play Book Assignment: Read James 3:3–6

Trash Talk

"My baby nephew dribbles better than you do!"

"Nice shirt. Didn't they have it in your size?"

"Is that your jump shot or are you having an attack?"

Trash talk. It gets a lot worse than that, but it's all over the place in sports. Even in leagues for kids your age. Even when you're just playing soccer in the backyard.

For some reason, a growing number of athletes can't be happy competing just by using their sports skill. They think they have to compete with their tongues.

One place this is really big is in the NBA, where a lot of talking goes on anyway. And these people aren't sharing recipes.

Not everyone is involved in trash talk, you know. Brent Price, who has played guard for Washington, Houston, and Vancouver, says, "I don't particularly like it. I don't try to partake in that. I was always taught that you go out, play hard, and keep your mouth shut. If you're going to do any damage, do it on the court, not with your mouth."

Probably one of the reasons Brent feels this way is that he is a Christian who knows that God has a lot of things to say about how we use our tongues.

God is pretty clear that what we say with our mouths shows what is inside our hearts. If there's a lot of trash rattling around in the heart, it'll make its way up to the old voice box. Then we cause some real damage.

Look at what God says about trash talk, just in the book of Proverbs:

- The wise in heart accept commands, but a chattering fool comes to ruin. (10:8)
- The mouth of the righteous is a fountain of life, but violence overwhelms the mouth of the wicked. (10:11)
- He who holds his tongue is wise. (10:19)
- A man who lacks judgment derides his neighbor, but a man of understanding holds his tongue. (11:12)
- An evil man is trapped by his sinful talk. (12:13)
- Reckless words pierce like a sword. (12:18)
- The mouth of the fool gushes folly. (15:2)

Do you know why the Bible says so much about our tongues and about how we should talk? It's because God, who made us, knows that controlling what we say is so very, very hard. And that we can do a lot of damage with it. Check out James 3.

Think of all the time your parents have spent speaking to you (maybe even throwing in a good lecture here and there) about how you talk. For most of us, it's not a matter of saying, "Oh, now I get it. I won't say any mean things anymore." It's a struggle that we must face every day.

And the only way to control what we say is by making sure our hearts are right with God. So before we talk to anyone each day, we need to talk with him and ask him to keep our tongue under control. Let God help us take the trash out of our talk.

On the Chalkboard

If you don't have anything nice to say, don't reveal it with words.

How about Un-Trash Talk?

Back when he was a minor-league player, Jack McKeon, who managed the Cincinnati Reds from 1997–2000, tried some reverse trash talk. A batter had swung and tipped McKeon's glove, which was interference on the catcher's part. The umpire made the right call and sent the batter to first base. McKeon decided to have some fun. He ripped off his mask and started yelling at the umpire. "That was a good call! I did tip the bat." The umpire was confused. This catcher was yelling at him, but he wasn't arguing. He was agreeing with him. McKeon continued. "I said it was a good call!" stomping his feet as he yelled. Finally, the befuddled umpire told McKeon to stop or he would throw him out of the game for delaying the game. He certainly couldn't throw him out for complimenting him! McKeon put his mask back on and returned to his position, satisfied to have had some fun with the umpire.

- - - - - - - - - - - - - - - - - - -*Instant Replay*

How do I trash-talk? Who do I trash-talk?
What can help me be a wise talker, not a wise guy?

Sports Stuff

There's another kind of talking that's good in sports. That is, talking to teammates. When you're on the field, there are lots of situations when you should talk. For instance, if you're an infielder in baseball or softball, you need to talk to your pitcher to encourage him or her. You need to talk to your other infielders to get in position and to know who is going to take the throw on the next play. In basketball, you have to talk to your teammates to tell them a pick is coming. And you have to communicate new plays and new defenses. You have to help your teammate if a player is coming up from behind. In all sports, you have to learn how to communicate with your teammates without being too talkative.

Whoever gives heed to instruction prospers.

Proverbs 16:20

Play Book Assignment: Read Ephesians 6:1–3

Why Bother with School?

How's school?

That's one subject everyone has an opinion about.

Some kids love it. Some, well, don't love it. Some just shrug their shoulders and say, "It's okay, I guess."

Even if you love school, sometimes it's hard to come up with a really good reason why you have to spend all those long hours in class.

Think about it. What difference does it makes that you can name all the states and capitals? Will you ever have to multiply mixed fractions in real life? Someday when you're a computer technician, will it matter that a cell has a nucleus? Or when you're in the middle of raising your kids in the far distant future, will it really matter that the tallest mountain in North America is Mount McKinley? And reelee, dus it madder if yu ken spel gud?

Of course, if you're planning on being a contestant on *Jeopardy!*, these things might come in handy. And that kind of knowledge sure helped the people on *Who Wants to Be a Millionaire?* But come on, is that any reason to study every night and do all that homework? Does a report on Peru make you a better person?

In other words, why study? Why mess with all that school stuff? Is God involved in that at all?

Perhaps. Let's look at two reasons why you might think so.

First, doing well in school is a good way to obey God when he talks about how to treat your parents. You know the verses in the Bible that say, "Honor your father and mother." Did you know that you honor them when you succeed in school?

Listen to A.C. Green, longtime NBA star. He says he didn't care much for good grades at first, but then something changed. He decided he should get good grades so he could honor his parents. "By the time I got to my junior year, my greatest goal was to be on the honor roll. I wanted my name on our school board that was right by the front door. I wanted to bring my parents in to see my name on that board. That made me work harder." It may seem weird to you now, but your success is a way of showing your parents how important they are to you. They want you to succeed, and when you do, they feel great.

A second reason to study is that God expects your best at all times. "Whatever you do, work at it with all your heart, as working for the Lord, not for men" (Colossians 3:23). If you play sports, you usually don't need this reminder. You're having so much fun running around out there, it's easy to do that with all your might. It comes naturally because you're having a great time.

But schoolwork is another ball game entirely. With school, you might need to remind yourself who you're doing this for. The best way to make sure you get the most out of the brain God gave you is to do your work for him, not for others.

There are two good reasons to hit the books: to honor your parents and to work for God.

Now, who was the thirty-seventh president of the United States?

On the Chalkboard

One good thing about an education is that it helps you realize you don't know everything.

A.C. Green's Principles

In A.C. Green's book *Victory*, he spells out fifty-two principles for living a godly life. One of those principles that deals with learning is number eight. It says, "Admit you don't know everything. Open yourself up to learn from others. Develop a teachable spirit."

- - - - - - - - - - - - - - - - - - -*Instant Replay*

What do I think of school? Have I ever thought about how my attitude toward learning and school reflects on my relationship with God?

Sports Stuff

More than a few students have missed out on playing varsity
sports because they didn't have good grades. If you want to
make sure you're ready to get the grades you need when
you're in high school sports, you need to start now to develop
good study habits. Do you keep an assignment book? Do you
make sure each assignment is complete each day? Do you
know how to study for tests? These things will help you in
school and in sports.

GAME PLAN

> That is why, for Christ's sake, I delight in weaknesses.... For when I am weak, then I am strong.
>
> 2 Corinthians 12:10

Play Book Assignment: Read 2 Corinthians 4:16—18

The Pain

What could be better than being a Major League Baseball player? When you go to work, you take a ball glove, not a lunch pail. Instead of slaving over a calculator figuring out a budget, you get to walk up to home plate with a baseball bat in your hand.

Your workday goes like this: go to a baseball park, put on a major league uniform, take batting practice, take fielding practice, play a game, talk to some reporters, take a shower, and go home.

That's your job!!

And you get millions of dollars for doing this.

Imagine, though, that your job is to be a professional athlete who has to be able to run fast, hit ninety-mile-an-hour fastballs, and play first base—all while suffering from arthritis.

Usually, we think of arthritis as being something Grandma has. But you may be like Rico Brogna, major-league first baseman. You may be young and have arthritis.

If you do, you know about the stiffness in your joints, about how hard it is to get out of bed in the morning, about how activity that is supposed to be fun for everyone else just makes the pain worse.

Rico Brogna, one of the best first basemen in the majors, has ankylosing spondylitis (AS), a type of arthritis that affects the bones and joints. Here's how he describes how AS slowed him down before he discovered what it was. "I tried to play with pain in my hips and spine. I walked like I was crippled, and I couldn't even bend over to tie my shoes."

Once he was diagnosed, the pain didn't go away, but he found out that exercise and medication could help.

But Rico has another source that helps him. He is a strong Christian who knows that even the problems with AS can have positive results. "It's during difficult times," he says, "that God brings me closer to himself. What I first thought was devastation has turned into an unbelievable blessing."

Whether you have arthritis or some other physical problem—or even if you have totally different tough problems—you can learn a lot from this baseball player.

God doesn't allow illness and trouble in our lives without giving us the strength to handle them and the hope that he has something better for us later.

So, don't give up when you're down. Lean on Jesus, as Rico Brogna does, and see what God can teach you.

On the Chalkboard

The real problem with pain is if we let it hurt our relationship with God.

Others Who Suffered

Several athletes have played at the highest levels despite serious illnesses. Baseball players Eric Davis and Andrés Galarraga both came back from cancer surgery and treatment.

The most famous is Lou Gehrig, a New York Yankee player of the 1920s and 1930s. He suffered from amyotrophic lateral sclerosis (ALS), which has become known as Lou Gehrig's disease.

- - - - - - - - - - - - - - - - - - -*Instant Replay*

What do I suffer from? How can I begin to trust God with my problem? How can it make me closer to God?

Sports Stuff

One advantage athletes have today over athletes of twenty or thirty years ago is that there are many more doctors who specialize in sports medicine now. Someone like Rico is able to play because doctors and therapists know how to treat him. If you have a sports-related injury, don't ignore it. If some part of your body is in pain for a long period of time (not just a sore muscle or a bruise), have someone check you over.

This is how God showed his love among us:

He sent his one and only Son into the world.

1 John 4:9

Play Book Assignment: Read 1 John 4:7–10

The Last Ball of the Century

The last baseball player to record a putout in the twentieth century was Chad Curtis of the New York Yankees. While playing left field for the Yankees in the 1999 World Series, Curtis caught the final out of game four of the series, which New York swept 4–0 over the Atlanta Braves.

When the Braves' last hitter flew out to Curtis to end the game, the series, and the century, Chad realized he had something very significant in his possession. So he squeezed the ball and made sure he took it with him. Even through the mad celebration that took place on the field, Chad hung on to that baseball. He intended to hold on to it as a keepsake.

That night, Chad climbed into his car and began the long drive home to Michigan. While driving through the night, he thought about that ball lying next to him on the passenger seat of the car. He decided that instead of keeping it for himself, he would give it to a friend in New York who had helped the Curtis family during the season.

Here's how Chad made that decision. He thought of God, who had someone very special with him in heaven. That special person was Jesus. God wanted to keep Jesus with him, but he also knew that he could help us by giving Jesus to us to die for us. So, with pain in his heart, God gave us Jesus.

Chad thought about that ball and decided that if God could give us Jesus, he shouldn't have any trouble giving his friend that baseball. So that's what he did.

Did you ever have something you didn't want to give up? Something special and close to your heart? Remember what it took for you to give that up? Imagine how it hurt God to send Jesus from perfect heaven to dusty, old, sinful earth. And to watch his Son die so horribly.

For Chad and for us, giving up a baseball is a tiny picture of what God did for us in sending Jesus as our Savior.

On the Chalkboard

We can never give up anything that comes close to what God gave up for our salvation.

Chad the Hero

Only six times in major-league history has anyone hit what is called a "walk-off" home run in the World Series. That means the home run is a late-inning winning run that wins the game, and both teams walk off the field without completing the inning. Three famous ones are Bill Mazeroski's 1960 blast that beat the New York Yankees in game seven that year, Kirk Gibson's ninth-inning home run to beat the Oakland A's in the 1988 series, and Joe Carter's ninth-inning home run that propelled the Toronto Blue Jays to their 1993 win over the Philadelphia Phillies. In 1999, Chad Curtis hit one of those. Batting in the tenth inning of game three, Chad blasted a round-tripper that gave the Yankees a 3–0 lead over the Braves. The next day, New York completed the sweep of the Braves, 4–0.

-Instant Replay

Have I ever thought of how God felt to see his Son crucified, knowing that his decision had sent Jesus to earth?

Sports Stuff

Hitting a home run isn't as easy as it looks. But you don't have to be as big as Mark McGwire to hit them. Chad is five foot ten and weighs 185 pounds. And the greatest home-run hitter in baseball history, Hank Aaron, wasn't a big person. The keys to Aaron's success (755 home runs) were quick hands and strong wrists. And great timing. The first key to good hitting is to coordinate all parts of the swing together. Other key factors include having a quick bat, getting the fat part of the bat on the ball, keeping your head from pulling away, and striding toward the pitcher's mound, not away from it.

GAME PLAN

Be devoted to one another in brotherly love.
Honor one another above yourselves.

Romans 12:10

Play Book Assignment: Read Matthew 26:34–36

The Ball Hog

"Throw it to me! Throw it to me!"

Everybody wants the ball during a basketball game, but there's only one to go around. That's why it's no fun at all to play on a team that has a ball hog on it.

Have you ever tried to play on a team that has a player like that? He or she dribbles, dribbles, and dribbles, trying to get open. Everybody else on the team is yelling, "Throw it to me!" But this person keeps the ball until he or she can get off a shot (or until the ball gets stolen).

Not everyone who has the ball a lot is a ball hog, of course. For instance, when Michael Jordan was still playing in the NBA, some people who didn't know the game said he was a ball hog. But he wasn't. He simply had the ball the most because he was the team's best player. He showed in a lot of ways that he cared for his teammates and wasn't out just for himself.

A ball hog doesn't know how to treat other people. A ball hog is selfish.

If we don't like ball hogs in basketball, we probably don't like ball hogs in regular life either. That means that we don't like to be around people who want all the attention and never think about others. And that means we need to be just the opposite of that. We need to be people who meet the needs of our friends instead of making sure only our needs are met.

In basketball, the needs of others might be as simple as getting them the ball. But in life, meeting needs includes things like protecting a friend who might be made fun of by others. Or giving up some free time to help someone who doesn't understand a subject you do understand. Or even warning a friend when he or she is about to do something wrong.

The only person who gets anything out of being selfish is the selfish person—and eventually the selfish person will get tired of being that way. Nobody likes a ball hog.

On the Chalkboard

A person wrapped up in himself makes a very small package.

Speaking of Shooting

Maybe these two players were just better than everyone else and weren't ball hogs, but for some reason they got almost all of the shots in the two games described:

In 1924, Marie Boyd scored 156 points in a basketball game. Playing for Lonaconing Central (Maryland), she helped her team beat Ursuline Academy 163–3.

In 1960, Danny Heater of Burnsville, West Virginia, scored 135 points in a boys' basketball game.

----------------------*Instant Replay*

As I think back over the past couple of days, were there some times I could have been more unselfish? What could I have done better?

Sports Stuff

To avoid being a ball hog in basketball, one thing to do is to become a better passer. First, you have to get really good at several kinds of basic passes: chest pass, bounce pass, baseball pass, hook pass. One way to do this by yourself is to find a solid wall and practice passing into the wall over and over and over. (If it's the basement wall, make sure your parents have earplugs.) As you get better, you can try passes like the behind-the-back pass.

GAME PLAN

Cast all your anxiety on him because he cares for you.

1 Peter 5:7

Play Book Assignment: Read 1 Peter 5:5–9

Bum Deal

One thing you'll probably have to put up with if you play sports is this: you'll get a bum deal somewhere along the way.

In other words, things won't always go your way.

You'll have a coach who doesn't seem to like you.

You'll have a game in which you don't play as much as you would like to play.

You'll have a referee's call go against you.

You'll slug the softball the hardest you've ever hit it, and some crummy outfielder will make the best catch she's ever made.

You'll climb into the car with Mom, who will drive you thirty-five minutes to the wrong field. And you'll finally arrive at the correct field with two minutes to go in the third quarter.

You'll have your best week of practice ever and then hurt your ankle in warm-ups before the big game.

This kind of stuff happens all the time to kids who play sports. They get bum deals. And they have to learn to deal with them in an unbum-like way.

Todd Walker is an infielder in the major leagues. Before he got a chance to play for the Minnesota Twins, he had his own series of bum deals.

One of the biggest bummers came when he began his rookie year in the major leagues. Walker had been an outstanding college player, and the year before he got to the major leagues, he was the Player of the Year in his level of the minor leagues. He was expected to become a big star.

But when he got to Minnesota, he stopped hitting. Through the first two months of his first season, his batting average was only .194. If you don't know how bad that is, it means that he was getting a base hit less than two times for every ten times he batted.

That's when he got some really bad news. On his twenty-second birthday, he received a note from the Twins that said he was being sent back down to the minors.

Be honest. What would you do if you got such bad news? Pout? Hit something? Yell and scream? Cry? Blame somebody?

Here's what Todd did. He trusted God.

"Was I mad at God?" he says. "No, not really. Sure, God could have allowed me to stay in the big leagues. But I think I learned a lot more by being sent down. You learn the most from your biggest failures. I looked to God for strength. The Bible says to put all your worries on the Lord, and that's what I try to do."

Now there's an idea. Try *that* the next time you get a bum deal.

Why get mad at God when trusting him is the way to succeed?

Getting to Know Todd Walker

Todd Walker has to have a rather large trophy case. It would have to hold his trophy for being the Louisiana High School Baseball Player of the Year in 1991. There would have to be room for his All-State plaque for soccer when he was in high school. Over in the corner could be the three awards he received for being all-American in baseball all three years he went to Louisiana State University. Not to mention having room for his 1992 NCAA Freshman of the Year award, his 1993 trophy for being the College World Series Player of the Year, and the award from *Baseball Digest* magazine, which named him the best collegiate second baseman between 1985 and 1994.

- - - - - - - - - - - - - - - - - - - -*Instant Replay*

What bum deal have I received recently?
How can I turn it into something that helps me
get closer to God, not further from him?

Sports Stuff

How you handle a tough spot in sports can make you or break you as an athlete. One of the best ways to practice making sure a disappointment on the court doesn't bother you is by not showing your emotions when a bad thing happens. When you play table tennis, for instance, practice staying calm whether you miss a shot or nail a winner. If you start training yourself not to get mad when you fail, you'll become a calmer player in all your sports.

We are therefore Christ's ambassadors.

2 Corinthians 5:20

Play Book Assignment: Read 2 Corinthians 5:16—20

Giving Hope

It's time for a little lesson in Español — Spanish.

If you already know the answer to this, be patient. Maybe another time you'll get a question that's more challenging.

Okay, here goes. What is the Spanish word for "hope"?

Is that your final answer?

Before we get to the answer, you need to read about a person who has found a way to give hope to some people in a poor country. The guy's name is Dave Valle, and he was at one time a catcher in Major League Baseball. He caught for the Seattle Mariners for several years and ended his career with the Texas Rangers. One year he was good enough to lead the American League in throwing out runners trying to steal bases.

Toward the end of his career, he and his wife, Vicki, decided that they wanted to do something to help people in the world who didn't have all the nice stuff they had. Quite a few years before, Dave had played some baseball in the Dominican Republic (you get ten extra points if you can point to it on a map). While there, he fell in love with the people, and he noticed that they didn't have much.

So, when Dave and Vicki thought of helping people, they decided to help Dominicans. And guess what they called their new ministry? They called it *Esparanza,* which means ... well, you know what it means.

Here's what the Valles did. They started a bank in the Dominican Republic that loans money to women. The women can then start their own small businesses with the money. In that way, the women have hope of earning a living. And, when the women get together at their "bank" meetings, someone tells them about Jesus Christ.

Do you ever think much about missionary work? About the work Christians do to take hope to people in other countries? Have you ever thought about how you might have a small part in helping missionaries and their work?

Dave and Vicki Valle realized that they were "Christ's ambassadors," so they found a way to give hope. Is what they are doing limited to adults? How can you give hope?

Could you support a child through World Vision or some other organization?

Could you put together a shoebox package for Samaritan's Purse?

Could you email a missionary family from your church and see if there's anything you can do to help them?

Could you help serve Thanksgiving dinner with your parents at a mission in your city?

Could you offer hope? Or *esperanza*? Of course you can. God gave you hope. Now share it.

On the Chalkboard

**When you have the hope of the world,
you have a responsibility to a hopeless world.**

Dominican Baseball

The country that Dave and Vicki Valle help has been one of the top sources for Major League Baseball players. One city, San Pedro de Macoris, Dominican Republic, has sent many players to the big leagues—including one very popular home-run hitter with a big smile, Sammy Sosa.

- - - - - - - - - - - - - - - - - - - -**Instant Replay**

**What is my impression of missionaries?
Could I ever see God using me in this way? Are there
any smaller things I should be doing now for missions?**

Sports Stuff

Dave Valle would admit it. He wasn't a very good hitter. Three times when he was in the majors, his batting average was below what they call the Mendoza Line: .200. So how did Valle stay in the majors for thirteen years? He was a specialist. Sometimes it pays to learn how to do one thing and do it very well. For Valle, one thing he did well was throw out runners.

So being a good defensive catcher helped him have a long career. What can you specialize in so your coaches will notice you and you can help the team? While working on all your skills, pick one thing and become an expert at it. Soccer: dribbling. Basketball: ballhandling. Baseball: bunting. Hockey: handling the stick. Specialize.

Those who live in accordance with the Spirit have their minds set on what the Spirit desires.

Romans 8:5

Play Book Assignment: Read Romans 8:5–8

You and Jesus

Suppose there was some kid in your class at school who was always doing stuff he shouldn't be doing. One day this guy calls you and says, "Hey, dude. I'm going over to the store to do some shoplifting. Want to come? I'm bringing my mom!"

Your mouth would drop open so fast, you might break your jaw.

Who takes their mom when they're going to do something they're not supposed to do. Kids who think it's cool to sneak out behind the bus garage at school and smoke don't ask the principal to join them. Who hauls Dad along when they go paint graffiti on the side of a building.

That'd be just dumb.

That's why the advice Jay Barker's parents gave him was so good. Jay used to be a quarterback at the University of Alabama. He was a good one too. In 1994, he finished fifth in the vote for the Heisman Trophy, an award given to the best college football player in the United States. And in his four years as quarterback of the Crimson Tide football team, Jay led Alabama to a record of thirty-five wins, two losses, and one tie. See? He was very good.

For Jay, though, being good didn't stop with football. He was a good person too. A dedicated Christian, he liked to speak to young people and remind them to stay pure for Jesus Christ. And one of the best ways he could explain to kids how to do that was to remind them of that really good advice his mom used to give him.

She told him, "If you are someplace where drinking is going on and people are wanting you to drink, just remember when you take a drink, Christ is taking it with you. Whatever you do, you are taking him with you. He isn't going to leave you while you are drinking or taking drugs."

See the point? Just as you'd feel really weird dragging your parents along when you were doing something wrong, you should feel weird knowing that when you do something that will harm you or your body or your testimony, you're dragging Jesus into it.

How can that be true? Look at these verses:

Jesus said, "I am with you always, to the very end of the age" (Matthew 28:20).

"Don't you know that you yourselves are God's temple and that God's Spirit lives in you?" (1 Corinthians 3:16).

One of the great things about trusting Jesus for salvation is that he comes to live within you in the person of the Holy Spirit. And one of the good things about that is that he can become a constant reminder to do things that are good and honorable.

So, it's you and Jesus. Where are you going now?

On the Chalkboard

If you're taking the King someplace, make sure it's nice.

Alabama Records

The Alabama football team has had some great quarterbacks. Among them were Joe Namath, who was the MVP of Super Bowl III for the New York Jets; Ken Stabler, who was a star for the Oakland Raiders; and Mike Shula, who is an NFL coach. But none of them had the stats Jay Barker had at Alabama. Playing from 1991 to 1994, he set school records for yards passing (5,689), completions (402), and most consecutive passes completed (11).

-Instant Replay

Have I taken Jesus anyplace recently where he probably didn't want to be taken? And did I do anything that I shouldn't have done with my body, Jesus' temple?

Sports Stuff

If you're really good at one sport, should you just stick to that one or play them all? When Jay Barker was little, he liked baseball, basketball, and football. He played them all in high school, although his best sport was football, and that's the one that got him a scholarship at Alabama. It's hard to decide whether to give up a sport to work on another one, but often it's best to continue playing multiple sports because even in high school it's hard to know which you'll be best at. This is one of those situations you and your parents need to talk about, because they can give you some great advice.

GAME PLAN

I call on the Lord in my distress, and he answers me.

Psalm 120:1

Play Book Assignment: Read Habakkuk 3:17–19

Take It from Matt

Matt Ware was one of those kids who don't come along very often at a small Christian high school. He was an exceptional basketball player for a tiny Christian high school. Like so many good, young players, he wanted to see how far his basketball skills would take him.

But one day in 1998, a possible career as a basketball player was taken away from him forever. While going for a loose ball in practice, Matt dove headfirst into a wall, breaking his neck. In a split second, he went from a sure-thing high school star and a possible college player to a kid whose future would be spent getting around in a wheelchair.

Take a few minutes to think about how you would respond to that kind of situation. Or maybe you've already gone through something like that. Think about the possible reactions a young teenager could have as he tries to figure out what the rest of his life would be like.

Would you be angry?

Would you be bitter?

Would you blame it on God?

Or could you possibly find a way to praise God through such a situation?

What Matt did after the accident and during the months that followed was remarkable. Soon after the injury, Matt recalled, he realized that "there's nothing I really could do but trust God. Your trust relies on God for what's gonna happen."

So the first thing Matt did was to keep trusting God. Before the accident, he had already put his saving faith in Jesus Christ. Now he was forced to put his living faith in him. And that's what he did.

The next remarkable thing Matt did was to understand that the difficulty he would be going through was something that could help him in his relationship with God. "Our weakness can help us stay closer to God," he said. "You can rely on him whenever a time of trouble comes."

How could Matt handle his situation with such faith? He had prepared for it ahead of time. No, he didn't know he would be paralyzed, but he did know how important it is to trust God every day and rely on him. Then, when trouble came, he was ready.

Are you still thinking about what you would do if a serious situation like Matt's ever happened to you? Do you think you're as close to God now as you would need to be if he was all you had to depend on? Are you ready to say what the writer of Habakkuk said—even if trouble comes I'll rejoice in God?

Matt was ready for anything because of his strong faith. Are you?

On the Chalkboard

Trusting God in the dark is easier if we practice by trusting him in the light.

More about Matt

Matt lives in Indianapolis, Indiana. When word got out about his injury, he was suddenly the subject of attention among some of basketball's best players and coaches. San Antonio Spurs' coach Gregg Popovich visited him and brought guard Avery Johnson with him. Matt was given signed sports stuff by the Indianapolis Colts, the Indiana Pacers, the Philadelphia 76ers, and the Purdue University Boilermakers. Even Michael Jordan sent Matt a signed basketball.

- - - - - - - - - - - - - - - - - - -*Instant Replay*

Would I be as brave as Matt? Even if I'm not a brave person by nature, what would make me able to handle something difficult like this?

Sports Stuff

Head injuries and spinal-cord injuries are among the most devastating sports injuries you can experience. Head injuries can be avoided by wearing protective headgear when you're roller blading or biking or playing sports like football. Sometimes (not in Matt's case), spinal-cord injuries happen because of carelessness. For instance, if you plan to dive into water, you always make sure the water is deep enough. If you play baseball or softball, be very cautious of diving headfirst—you may run into the fielder's leg. And if you play football, avoid spearing with your helmet. Play hard, but play carefully.

GAME PLAN

What is more, I consider everything a loss compared to the surpassing greatness of knowing Christ Jesus my Lord.

Philippians 3:8

Play Book Assignment: Read John 3:1–8

Do You Know Him?

Do you mind a little bit of a personal story? I hope not, because I'm going to tell it anyway.

When I was in college, there was a basketball player who many people said was the most exciting player who ever played college basketball. Those people didn't get any arguments from me. His name was Pete Maravich, and he played hoops for Louisiana State University.

You might want to ask your mom or dad about him—or your grandparents. If they saw him play, they will know what I'm talking about when I say he played basketball like no one else ever.

Pistol Pete was a guard who averaged forty-four points a game throughout his entire college basketball career. Forty-four points! And that was before the three-point line had been invented.

But it wasn't just his shooting that was absolutely incredible. He was also an unbelievable ballhandler. He passed the ball in ways people didn't think possible. And his dribbling antics made the guys guarding him look stupid.

Here's just one example. He could be running full steam downcourt and throw a perfect between-the-legs, behind-the-back pass to a teammate. At full speed right-handed, he would dribble between his legs, pick up the ball with his left hand, and whip a perfect behind-the-back peg to a fellow Tiger streaking down the right side of the court.

Okay, Pete was my hero. I had pictures of him all over my wall. I wore my socks in the same baggy style he did. I got my hair cut like his. I paid money to watch him play. I imitated his moves (the ones I could figure out). I tried to shoot my jump shot like his. I wanted to be Pete Maravich.

But despite all that, I never knew him. I may have known more about him than most other people, but I never met him.

He died in 1988 before I ever had a chance to meet him or interview him.

Why do I tell you this about me and Pete?

Because you may be that way with Jesus. You may know tons about him. You may go to his "house" every Sunday. You may even read about him in the Bible. You may really admire him and even want to live like he did — being kind and caring for others.

But you can know all that without knowing Jesus at all.

Do you know Jesus? Have you met him by putting your faith in his death on the cross for you? Have you asked him to be your Savior, which means you can then talk with him and develop a real relationship with him?

Please don't do like I did with Pete. Before I got a chance to meet him, it was too late. Make sure you get to know Jesus Christ before you don't have a chance to anymore.

Meet Jesus. Really get to know him.

On the Chalkboard

Knowing about Jesus is no substitute for knowing him.

More about Pete

Pete Maravich played ten years in the NBA. One year, he led the league in scoring, with thirty points a game. But all the time he played, he knew he was missing something. When he was eighteen, he had rejected the opportunity to trust Jesus as his Savior. When he was in his midthirties, he finally realized how important it is to become a Christian. After getting saved, Pete was a great evangelist. He went around the country telling young basketball fans that despite having earned millions of dollars and becoming incredibly famous, the best thing that happened to him was becoming a Christian. He died on January 5, 1988, while playing pickup basketball with Dr. James Dobson of Focus on the Family.

- - - - - - - - - - - - - - - - - - - -*Instant Replay*

Am I sure I know Jesus? Who can I talk with to help me if I have doubts?

Sports Stuff

Before Pete Maravich died, he produced a series of basketball videos called *Homework Basketball*. One of the things he emphasized in those videos was the importance of doing drills. If you want to spend the time it takes to get better at your sport, you need to repeat certain skills over and over and over. With basketball, doing dribbling and ballhandling drills are essential. They help you handle the ball like it's second nature. In baseball, you can break down fielding your position into sections and work on each part of fielding with drills (for instance, practice fielding ground balls and making the transfer of ball to glove to throwing position). You can always develop your own drills for the sport you play.

He who sows righteousness reaps a sure reward.

Proverbs 11:18

He who sows wickedness reaps trouble.

Proverbs 22:8

Play Book Assignment: Read Galatians 6:7–10

Throwing It All Away

This guy was good!

He could catch passes most people didn't even wave at. Opposing players looked like high school kids next to this college star.

Mr. Hands (not his real name) was such a good receiver that most people were ready to give him the Heisman Trophy without even voting on it. There was no doubt he was the best player in the land. And the land had a bunch of good players.

But then our hero forgot something. He didn't forget to run the right routes for his quarterback. He didn't forget how to wrap his strong fingers around the pigskin.

He forgot one of God's laws.

You know this law. It's the one your parents might remind you about when you don't turn in your homework. Or when you try to sneak around and do something you aren't supposed to.

It's the law from God that says, "Whatever you sow, that's what you'll reap." If you plant corn in your garden, don't expect to come back in two months and pick tomatoes. And if you plant sin, don't expect to turn around and find God blessing you.

The Heisman Trophy candidate forgot the law when he went into a store and walked out with hundreds of dollars of merchandise that he didn't pay for. Of course, he also forgot to check for a store security camera, which caught the deed on tape—but that's another story.

As a result of stealing these clothes, the football star was dropped from consideration for the Heisman Trophy. He sowed dishonesty, and he reaped embarrassment. He gained some new clothes, but he lost some pretty impressive hardware.

God wasn't kidding. He meant it when he had Paul write this verse: "Do not be deceived: God cannot be mocked. A man reaps what he sows" (Galatians 6:7).

Do you know how much God cares for you? He cares enough to let you know how things work in his world. He doesn't make up stuff after we do it and say, "Ha! Ha! I caught you." No, he says, "Listen, my child. Let me give you some help. If you do bad things, other bad things will follow. But if you do good things, you will be honored." Sowing. Reaping. It's pretty clear.

The football player knew that. But he thought just this once he could sneak by without consequence. Bad idea for him.

Bad idea for you. God loves you, and he wants what's best. Listen to what he tells you.

If you go looking for trouble, it will find you.

Heisman Talk

Here are some people who won the Heisman Trophy, with an interesting fact about each.

Charlie Ward, 1993. Never drafted by the NFL, so he went on to play in the NBA for the New York Knicks.

Danny Wuerffel, 1996. Played for the New Orleans Saints. Started the *Our Daily Bread* club—teammates who would read the devotional booklet *Our Daily Bread* every day.

Barry Sanders, 1988. Retired from football while just short of breaking the all-time record for rushing yards.

Archie Griffin, 1974, 1975. Only player who ever won the Heisman Trophy twice.

- - - - - - - - - - - - - - - - - - -*Instant Replay*

Do I realize that my parents love me when they try to help me avoid trouble—even though I think they are too strict? Do I realize they are trying to do what God wants them to?

Sports Stuff

Does it matter to your team what you do when you're not with them? Lots of athletes are finding out that it does. First, when you aren't with the team it's a good time to work on things that will make you a better player. Second, many athletes make wrong decisions when they're out on their own.

They might get hurt doing something foolish, or they might get in trouble. In either case, these athletes let their teammates down because they can't participate as they should.

So remember that you are always a part of the team, even when the team isn't with you.

Pray continually.

1 Thessalonians 5:17

Play Book Assignment: Read Romans 1:8–10

Smart As a Football Player

The quarterback drops back to pass. It's a blitz! He runs to his right. He looks up. He fires the ball downfield. His wide receiver has his man beat! The receiver reaches up. He makes the catch! He's at the twenty. The ten. The five. Touchdown!

You're watching the game on your TV at home, and you see the wide receiver do something the TV announcer doesn't mention. The player who just scored the TD crosses the goal line, stops, points up into the air, and then kneels on one knee and prays.

What's going on here?

This display of faith isn't welcomed by everyone. Some people don't like football players bringing their faith onto the field by praising God and then praying after scoring a touchdown. And some people who appreciate prayer may even have a question about what such a prayer says. Does it suggest that God cares for one person over another?

No matter what other people think about this practice, it does mean one thing for sure. The athlete who scored the touchdown realizes that prayer can happen anywhere. And he may even be trying to live out this important biblical teaching: "Pray continually" (1 Thessalonians 5:17).

Ever wonder what in the world that verse means? Does it mean that we can do only one thing in life: pray? Does it mean we can't eat, sleep, wash the dishes (you wish), study (you double wish), or enjoy a good game of tiddlywinks? Are we supposed to be monks sitting around all day chanting prayers?

To find out what it means, look at Romans 1:8−10. In those verses, Paul (a very active guy, who although he wasn't a football player, was definitely not a monk) said that his continual prayer went like this: "Constantly I remember you in my prayers at all times" (v. 9). It means that as he did other things, he kept prayer requests for his Roman friends in mind. Then he could pray for them regularly.

Think back over your day today or yesterday. How often did you pray? Was it continual? Was it regular?

For some football players, crossing the goal line has become a reminder to pray.

You can develop reminders. For instance, take a Post-it note packet and write some requests on the pages. Then stick them on your textbooks. When you open your book bag and find the note that says, "Mom's job problems," you'll remember to pray a quick prayer for your mom. Or stick some on your mirror in your room. Then, when you're fooling with your hair, you'll have a reminder to pray.

You can be as smart as a football player. If one of them can make it a habit to talk to God with sixty-thousand people watching, you can develop a similar habit in your life.

It's a great way to obey the verse that says, "Pray continually."

On the Chalkboard

No matter what you're doing, God is listening. Pray often.

Speaking of Praying

In the mid-1990s, the National Collegiate Athletic Association (NCAA) tried to stop players from praying in the end zone after a touchdown. However, a lot of people said that wasn't fair and fought the rule. The NCAA decided it was a bad rule and threw it out.

- - - - - - - - - - - - - - - - - - -*Instant Replay*

How many times do I usually pray in a day? Could I double that? Triple it? Not to show off but to help my relationship with God.

Sports Stuff

On the sports teams you have played on, is it popular to be a Christian? Sometimes, even on teams made up of all Christians, teammates will make you feel funny if you try to stand up for Jesus. Yet God has put you on that team for a reason, and it's not to teach you to hide your faith. Being careful not to make a scene, be strong in your faith — even in sports.

GAME PLAN

> Devote yourselves to prayer, being watchful and thankful.
>
> Colossians 4:2

Play Book Assignment: Read Ephesians 3:14–21

The Circle of Prayer

Did you ever hit, grab, slug, tackle, pound, snarl at, and try to defeat someone and then turn around and pray with that person? Did you ever kneel down and hold hands in prayer with someone you just spent the last sixty minutes running into, knocking over, and butting heads with?

If you were a football player in the NFL, you could possibly answer yes to both of those questions.

Have you ever noticed what happens when an NFL game is over? Of course the coaches race across the field to shake each other's hand, and the TV people grab the star of the game for a quick interview. But there's something else.

Players from both sides meet at midfield, kneel down on the surface, hold hands, and pray.

Sound strange?

Some people think it is. They can't figure out how it can happen. And why.

Although not everyone agrees that it's a good idea, there is something we can learn from Circle Prayer, as it's sometimes called.

First, praying with someone is a great way to overcome differences. Football players may work hard to beat the other team, but those who are Christians can set all that aside when the game is over and focus on what they have in common: love for God.

Second, praying is a way of witnessing about faith in God. Just as your family can witness to others when your dad thanks God for your food in a restaurant, these players are declaring that they believe in God and his power to answer their prayers.

Third, being a strong, tough athlete doesn't mean you don't trust God. Sometimes people think that a tough athlete can't be a strong Christian — that Christians are too meek. But the huge number of Christians who testify to their faith in God through Circle Prayer proves that is wrong.

So, how does this have anything to do with you?

Is there someone you have a disagreement with? Pray with him or her.

Are you bold enough and confident enough in your belief in God to pray in public? At school? At McDonald's?

Do you know that everyone needs to trust God, even the strongest people?

You can learn a lot from watching pro football. Even after the game is over.

On the Chalkboard

One of the best things about prayer is what it says about the person who prays.

Speaking of Circle Prayer

There are a couple of stories around that tell how Circle Prayer was started. One story comes from Howard Cross, a longtime tight end for the New York Giants. He said that he and some friends started getting together for prayer after their college games when he was at the University of Alabama. Then, a couple of years after he joined the NFL, he and the Giants' chaplain, David Bratton, decided to try it in the pros.

- - - - - - - - - - - - - - - - - - -*Instant Replay*

How important is prayer in my life? Are there some obstacles that stop me from praying? How can I be as strong as an NFL player when it comes to prayer?

Sports Stuff

Some people say athletes shouldn't be friends in any way with the players on the other team. One famous basketball player used to say that when teams play each other in the NBA finals, they have to hate each other. That isn't a good approach. To be a good competitor, you need to be focused on what you should be doing, on the techniques and strategies of the other team, and on keeping yourself mentally sharp. If you start to focus on your feelings for the other team, you will be wasting valuable mental effort. You don't need to hate opponents to beat them.

GAME PLAN

Teach me to do your will, for you are my God.

Psalm 143:10

Play Book Assignment: Read Ephesians 5:8–17

Living Like a Point Guard

Do you like to play basketball?

Would you make a good point guard? Can you handle the pressure of someone trying to steal the ball from you while you're setting up the next play? Do you think you can make the right passes and dribble the ball well enough to beat a full-court press? Are you enough of a leader to make sure all four other players are doing the right thing? The point-guard position is a tough one because it leads to a lot of pressure and gives you tons of chances to mess up.

Being a point guard is good practice for life. In life, you have to make good decisions just like a point guard does. And you are trying to do what someone else is directing you to do. With a basketball team, it's the coach. In life, it's God.

Have you ever heard of the phrase "doing God's will"? As the point guard of your own life, that's what you're trying to do every day. You're trying to make decisions and do things that God wants you to.

So, how can you know what God wants you to do? What is his game plan for you?

In the locker room before a game, sometimes the coach will write the keys to winning on the board. These are his "will" for the game. By looking through the Bible, we can pull out God's will for life. If we were putting them on the locker-room board, we'd write something like this:

1. "Give thanks in all circumstances" (1 Thessalonians 5:18).
2. "Be sanctified," or set apart as special (1 Thessalonians 4:3).
3. Don't be conformed to the world (Romans 12:2).
4. Do good things. This will keep foolish people quiet (1 Peter 2:15).

It's not always easy to be the point guard of your own life, trying to do what God wants you to do. But it's worth the effort. Just as a team plays a lot better when the point guard does what the coach says, your life will be more successful if you do as God says.

Get the point?

On the Chalkboard

When you are trying to live for God, the best power to use is "will" power.

Point Guards to Follow

The NBA has had some very good point guards who were Christians. In the mid- and late nineties, two of the best were Mark Price and Kevin Johnson. Others have been Brent Price, Bryce Drew, Avery Johnson, Charlie Ward, and Elliot Perry.

These men not only knew how to lead their teams, but they also knew how to live their lives for God.

-------------------Instant Replay

What decisions did I make recently without even asking God what he thought?

Sports Stuff

If you want to be a successful point guard, you have to have certain characteristics and skills.

First, you have to be a very good ballhandler. This means spending hours and hours dribbling and passing so you can have complete confidence in yourself.

Second, you have to be able to see the entire floor, not just the players near you. You have to notice when your teammates get open and when they need to be redirected.

Third, you have to learn to be a coach on the floor. You have to know the plays better than anyone else does, and you have to be able to be bold enough to tell your teammates what they are supposed to be doing.

We put up with anything rather than hinder the gospel of Christ.

1 Corinthians 9:12

Play Book Assignment: Read Luke 6:42

Bill and Faith

At one time, Bill Bradley was one of the best basketball players in the country. He led his team, Princeton, to some very exciting victories. Later, he played for the New York Knicks, where he was on an NBA championship team.

When he was in college, he was quoted by some publications as saying he was a Christian. He made it clear that he believed the gospel of Jesus Christ.

Something happened to Bradley through the years that changed his mind. Although it's tough to talk about because we hate to see anyone reject the faith, we can learn from the reasons he gave for turning his back on Christianity.

One of the key things he didn't like was what he called hypocrisy in the church. Do you know what hypocrisy is?

It's when Christians say they are one thing and yet act another way completely.

Like when a preacher speaks out against a certain sin and then gets caught committing that sin.

Or when a church member stands up and says we have to be honest and then gets thrown in jail for taking money from the company he works for.

Or when we say we love everybody, but we talk about our friends as if they're our worst enemy. "Hey, did you see Trevor's new shirt? It looks like he got it at a garage sale."

There are lots of people who think the way Bill Bradley thinks. They don't like the way some Christians behave, and they decide they don't want to be associated with us.

We can learn a couple of things from this former basketball player.

First, we shouldn't be hypocrites. We should be true to our word about who we are. Remember that Jesus didn't like hypocrisy. He said, "Woe to you, teachers of the law and Pharisees, you hypocrites!" (Matthew 23:27). And Peter, writing directly to Christians, said, "Rid yourselves of all malice and all deceit, hypocrisy, envy, and slander" (1 Peter 2:1). Someone like Bill Bradley shouldn't be able to find hypocrites in the church. Notice what Paul said: "We put up with anything rather than hinder the gospel" (1 Corinthians 9:12). And being a hypocrite can hinder the gospel.

Second, even if there are hypocrites in the church, that doesn't change the gospel. Jesus' message of hope and forgiveness is what we need to remember. We trust Jesus because of who he is, not because of who the people in the church are.

There will always be people like Bill Bradley — people who are searching for answers but who miss the true answer because of something that draws their attention away from Jesus.

Let's make sure we aren't distracting anyone from Jesus. Let's keep pointing to him. He's the only answer!

On the Chalkboard

People will fail us and disappoint us, but Jesus never fails.

One Big Game for Bradley

Bill Bradley was the Player of the Year in college basketball in 1965. In his final game as a collegian, he went out with a bang. Playing against Wichita State University in the consolation game of the Final Four (the NCAA doesn't play this game anymore), Bradley set a Final Four record with 58 points as Princeton beat Wichita State 118–82.

- - - - - - - - - - - - - - - - - - -**Instant Replay**

When my friends look at me, do they see Jesus or someone who distracts them from Jesus?

Sports Stuff

Bill Bradley was one of the best pure shooters in college basketball history, and his deadly accuracy was the result of long, long hours of practice. The story is told that one time when he was warming up for a college game, he thought he noticed that the rims were just a bit too low. Maybe less than a quarter of an inch. So, he mentioned it to his coach. Sure enough, when someone measured the rim before the game, it was discovered to be off by exactly what Bradley said. That kind of eye for the basket comes only through hour after hour of shooting practice. And it points out the importance of making sure the basket you practice on is exactly ten feet from the ground.

It is God who arms me with strength.

Psalm 18:32

Play Book Assignment: Read Isaiah 40:30—31

Real Strength

How strong are you?

There are lots of ways to measure strength.

You can measure your strength by the number of push-ups you can do.

Or the amount of weight you can bench press.

Or the number of chin-ups you can do.

With some athletes, you can tell how strong they are just by looking at them. You can see their rippling muscles. Or you can watch them do stuff you know takes a lot of strength and power.

Think of how strong you have to be to be a gymnast. There's the floor routine with its handstands and flips and huge flying-through-the-air acrobatics. There's the balance beam, which requires you to do all sorts of stuff while making sure you don't crash down on your head. There are the uneven parallel bars, with all that swinging and catching yourself and looping around at crazy angles.

Did you ever look at gymnasts' arms? They have pipes!

One of the best gymnasts who ever lived was Mary Lou Retton. In 1984, Mary Lou performed one of the most memorable and awe-inspiring feats in gymnastics history. She was in the running for the all-around championship in women's gymnastics at the Olympics, but she was slightly behind a woman from Eastern Europe going into the final event, the vault.

She would need a perfect vault to win.

With a look of sheer determination, she flung herself toward the vault. She leaped from the springboard, vaulted herself high into the air, turned perfectly, and landed with an absolutely flawless landing. She had stuck a perfect 10.

The event was being held in Los Angeles, and the crowd went crazy. Mary Lou had captured the gold medal.

Today, Mary Lou is a wife, a mother, and a strong Christian. And she recognizes the value of strength. She says, "Physical strength comes from training, lifting one more weight. Or in the case of a gymnast, doing one more flip."

But then Mary Lou makes an observation that is very important to you even if you've never, ever tried to do a reverse flip off the balance beam: "But real courage and real strength comes from God."

Are you any good at memorizing? There's a passage in Isaiah 40 that you need to memorize. It talks about the fact that even someone as young as you gets tired, and then it talks about how a tired person can get strength. Real strength. The kind Mary Lou is talking about.

The verses go like this: "Even youths grow tired and weary, and young men stumble and fall; but those who hope in the Lord will renew their strength" (vv. 30–31).

How strong are you? That all depends on how much you depend on God. He alone can give you real strength—strength of heart and soul.

Feeling weak? Put your hope in the Lord. Then you'll be as strong as Mary Lou! (Although you may not get a gold medal in the Olympics.)

On the Chalkboard

You are only as strong as your relationship with the Lord.

Speaking of Medals

The US women's all-around team was in a similar circumstance in the 1996 Olympic Games in Atlanta. The US team needed a good vault from Kerri Strug to win the first-ever US women's all-around gold medal. Despite an injured ankle, Kerri landed a very good vault, giving the team the gold medal.

- - - - - - - - - - - - - - - - - - -Instant Replay

How strong am I spiritually? How can I get stronger?

Sports Stuff

Does size matter in sports? Of course, you can't play center for the New York Liberty if you are five foot two, but sometimes it doesn't matter. Mary Lou Retton was only four foot nine inches tall and weighed just ninety-two pounds when she became a world-class athlete. What made the difference for her was dedication. She devoted her time to gymnastics and even moved away from home to dedicate herself totally to it. Although that kind of commitment isn't needed for most sports, it does suggest how much a person has to give up to become the best. What are you willing to set aside to become a better athlete? That's a question you have to ask if you want to be a champion.

Consider it pure joy, my brothers, whenever you face trials of many kinds.

James 1:2

Play Book Assignment: Read James 1:2–8

Getting Out of Trouble

Did you ever have one of those tough days that never seems to end? You know the kind.

Your mom wakes you up five minutes before the bus comes. You leave your homework on the dining-room table. Some kindergarten kid drips stuff from his drink box on your science book. Attila the Sub is behind the desk when you walk into the classroom. And you find a note in your locker from your best friend telling you she's now your former best friend.

You know. Worst-case scenario stuff.

Did you know that professional golfers can have nothing-ever-goes-right-for-me days too? Take it from Jackie Gallagher-Smith. It can happen.

Now, you probably haven't heard of Jackie. She's not nearly as famous as Tiger Woods or even Annika Sorenstam — but then who is? But Jackie is a golfer who has been earning a living at it since 1994. In 1999, she won her first major tournament, the Sony Open.

But Jackie has also had her share of trouble on the tour too. She's had days that are like that really-crummy-I-hate-life kind of day described above.

Like a January day in 1997. Jackie had worked hard to win the right to play on the pro tour. As with all pros, she had to qualify the previous autumn in a pressure-packed tournament. After missing a year of tour play because she didn't qualify (1996), she was back.

So what happened? On the first hole of the first tournament in 1997, she was attempting to hit the ball out of a bunker when she caught the club on the lip of the trap and injured her right hand. It would be several months before her hand would return to normal.

One thing Jackie has learned through this and other tough breaks in golf is that she needs to have a plan for keeping her head up when bad things happen. Here is her five-step plan:

1. *Remember that God loves you no matter what*. Even if you just flunked a math test, God still loves you.
2. *Count your blessings*. Sure it's a rotten day, but you're still breathing. There's food in the fridge. Your dog still loves you.
3. *Get into the Bible and pray*. The Bible is still true, and God is still listening.

4. *Talk to someone who cares.* That's one reason God gave you parents.

5. *Think about heaven.* The good stuff is on the way.

Having a tough day? Take Jackie's advice. It works.

On the Chalkboard

No day is so bad that God can't make it good.

Goofy Golf

Here's an idea you might use if you're having a little trouble improving your golf game. In 1975, a guy named Joe Flynn took on the six-thousand-yard-long Port Royal Golf Course in Bermuda in a unique way. He left his golf clubs in the car and threw the ball. His score? An 82 for eighteen holes. Hmmmm. Worth a try.

-Instant Replay

Have I ever stopped to consider that there are millions of people in the world worse off than I am on my very worst day?

Sports Stuff

If you are just getting started with golf, here a few tips that might help:

1. *Getting clubs.* A good starter set would be a putter; numbers 3, 5, 7, and 9 irons, plus numbers 1 and 3 woods.

2. *Getting started.* It would be best to take golf lessons so someone can teach you the best grips, strokes, and stances. Also, you'll need advice on which clubs to use when.

3. *Learning etiquette.* Golfers are expected to follow a set of guidelines for polite behavior. This includes how to care for the course, how to use the green without damaging it, and who hits first on each lie (the position of a ball that has come to a stop).

4. *Learning the rules.* Sometimes this comes by playing, but it's good to be familiar with the basic rules before getting on the course.

> Neither height nor depth, nor anything else in all creation, will be able to separate us from the love of God that is in Christ Jesus our Lord.
>
> Romans 8:39

Play Book Assignment: Read Romans 8:28–39

Good News or Bad?

Let's say you're playing on your school soccer team. You have a big game coming up next Friday. On Thursday at practice, you pull your leg back to boot the ball downfield, but when you come down to kick, your big toe finds a rock that is jutting out of the ground.

You fall to the ground and grab your toe while your teammates all gather around to see how you're doing. As soon as you can, you get back up, but you can't walk. The toe hurts too much. You suddenly realize that you might not be able to play in tomorrow's game.

Is this good news or bad?

Although that seems as easy to answer as the first question on *Who Wants to Be a Millionaire?*—(Mary had a little _____ (a) headache; (b) Boy Blue; (c) lamb; (d) sports car) it's not that easy.

Of course, it seems to be bad news. After all, you've been practicing for this game, and your team needs you.

But there's another way to look at it.

That's what Ruthie Bolton-Holifield discovered one year when she hurt her shoulder. Ruthie is a star basketball player who played for the US Olympic team and in the WNBA. She has long been considered one of the best women basketball players in the United States.

She's had her share of injuries, including a messed-up shoulder. When she injured her shoulder, her first thought was that she couldn't believe it, and she wondered what she did wrong to deserve this.

But then she decided to look at it another way. Here's how: "Sometimes God allows things to happen to test you, as he did with Job. My favorite Bible verse is Romans 8:39. It says that nothing can separate us from the love of God—not trials or tribulations or the difficulties and obstacles that come our way—nothing. When things get tough, I remind myself that God is in control of my career and my life. He knows what's best."

That's turning something bad into something good. Ruthie understands that even when a bad thing happens, it points out God's goodness and control. And that's good.

On the Chalkboard

Looking for God's good in bad situations helps heal the hurt.

The Women's US Olympic Team

The US team Ruthie Bolton-Holifield played on in the 1996 Olympics in Atlanta was perhaps the best women's basketball team ever. The squad not only played in the games in Atlanta, but also in an entire year of games in preparation for the Olympics. While barnstorming around the world, the team didn't lose a single game. Many of those players formed the backbone of the WNBA when it began in 1997.

- - - - - - - - - - - - - - - - - - -*Instant Replay*

What situation am I going through that I think is bad but really is good because it's teaching me about God?

Sports Stuff

One of the reasons Ruthie Bolton-Holifield became such a good basketball player was that she grew up in a family with lots of brothers and sisters. That meant she always had good competition to play against. She and her sisters—including Mae Ola, who had a tryout in the WNBA—spent a lot of time playing against their brothers. It's always good to practice and play games against players stronger and better than you. So as you try to improve your skills, look for some tough competition to practice against. It'll make you a better player.

Now the body is not made up of one part but of many.

1 Corinthians 12:14

Play Book Assignment: Read 1 Corinthians 12:12–26

All Goalies, All the Time

"All right! Everybody over here!"

It's Coach Pierre of your hockey team.

"Before we go out on the ice, let me go over your positions for today's scrimmage.

"Van Dyke, you're playing goalie.

"Robinson, you're my goalkeeper.

"Keller, why don't you be keeper today?

"Jefferson, I want you in goal."

You and your teammates look at each other. Has this guy flipped? You can't all play goalie!

Who would shoot on the other end of the ice? Who would take the face-offs? Who would slam the other players into the boards?

It's kind of a ridiculous situation, isn't it?

But it's a lot like what the apostle Paul was talking about when he told the Corinthian church about the jobs God gives people to do.

The main difference was that he was using the body as the illustration, not hockey. (Paul wasn't into hockey, apparently.) And what he was trying to point out was that we Christians all have different jobs to do.

Have you ever spent any time thinking about what God wants you to do? What role does he want you to have among Christians?

You may think you're too young to know what God wants you to do, but that's not true. Even if you think only about the different things kids your age can do for God, you should begin to learn that not everyone can do the same thing. God has given you a specific skill or gift that you can use for him now.

For example, maybe you're good with a musical instrument. Or perhaps you're a good actor. Maybe you have a lot of Bible knowledge. Or you could be one of those friendly people who has no trouble meeting new people or making friends. It could be something totally different.

When you begin to notice how different your interests and skills are from others, you'll see to see what Paul was talking about. God made each of us differently because he has such a wide variety of things that need to be done.

Just as a hockey coach needs some kids to play center, some to play wing, some to play forward, and some to play goalie, so God has us pegged for different jobs in the church.

Begin now to see what God wants you to do for him.

On the Chalkboard

The only person who can fill your spot on God's team is you.

Speaking of Goalies

Sometimes goalies have it easy. Sometimes they are really, really busy. Sam LoPresti of the Chicago Blackhawks had one of those busy nights on March 4, 1941. While playing against the Boston Bruins, LoPresti was bombarded by eighty-three shots by the Bruins. When the ice chips had cleared, he had given up just three goals. Boston won 3–2.

-Instant Replay

What do I think God has in mind for me? What are a couple of things I'm good at?

Sports Stuff

In sports, it can be to your advantage to learn other positions on the team. Sometimes, for instance, a basketball player may need to know how to play the 1, 2, and 3 positions. If the player can play all three, the coach can put him or her into any of those spots. Study what the other players do; don't learn just your position. It'll make you a better all-around player and give you more of a chance to get in the game.

Do not follow the crowd in doing wrong.

Exodus 23:2

Play Book Assignment: Read 2 Chronicles 13:4—7

Bad Company

The star basketball player (we'll call him Slim) grew up going to church, went to a Christian school through the eighth grade, and had parents who tried to teach him how to live for God.

By the time he graduated from high school, this young star was one of the best players in his state. He was recruited by colleges all over the country.

When Slim finally decided what school to go to, he was joined by several other high school stars. The college team was expected to become national champions because it had so many good players.

At college, Slim was a star. When he teamed up with the other really good players, they became a nationwide power-house.

But all wasn't great for Slim. His new teammates didn't want anything to do with his beliefs or his faith. They started getting him interested in parties and hangin' out and doing anything but living for Jesus Christ.

The bigger he got as a star, the less he thought about his faith. After college, he went on to the NBA, where he spent the first several years of his career building a reputation as a troublemaker, as somebody coaches didn't want, and even as someone who got into trouble with the law.

Reflecting on the path Slim took, his youth pastor from his high school days said simply, "He got in with the wrong crowd, and they led him astray."

What happened to Slim can happen to any Christian. Notice what Paul said in 1 Corinthians 15:33: "Bad company corrupts good character." He was talking specifically about how a per-son who has wrong beliefs can influence someone with right beliefs to change, but the verse also shows what happens when we hang around with people who aren't godly.

You probably see this happen at school a lot. A new kid comes to your school. You can tell he's trouble, so you stay away from him. But a friend thinks he's cool, so he starts doing stuff with the guy. Before you know it, you're saying to your friend, "What are you doing with that guy? You never used to _____ [fill in your own bad habit], but now you do."

It happened to Rehoboam thousands of years ago (2 Chron-icles 13:7), and it can happen to you. Don't let it. Don't let bad company make you do bad things.

A friend who leads you to do wrong is no friend at all.

Speaking of Influence

Did you know that in most major sports leagues, there is a group of people who are trying to be a good influence on the athletes? They're chaplains. They hold chapel services and Bible studies for the players of the NBA, NFL, Major League Baseball, and the WNBA. This has been a really good influence on a lot of players, because they have someone they can go to and ask for prayer or advice about tough situations.

-------------------*Instant Replay*

How can I tell whether I'm influencing a person for good, or that person is influencing me for bad? Who can help me with this?

Sports Stuff

Some athletes have a hard time understanding that their behavior off the field or court or ice can affect their sport. Here are some ways it can, and what you can do about it:

1. *Grades.* Many good athletes can't play because they don't have the grades. What to do: Keep up on your daily assignments. Get into the habit of reading. Get help knowing how to study for tests.
2. *Discipline.* What you do in the classroom or even outside of class will affect how your coach looks at you. What to

do: as a Christian, you can't do better than wear a WWJD bracelet to remind you of what Jesus would do.

3. *Attitude.* If you have a chip on your shoulder (if you don't know what this means, it probably means no one has ever accused you of having one, and you probably don't), coaches won't want you around. What to do: stop thinking that everyone is trying to get you. Think: "They are trying to help me. What do I need to learn?"

GAME PLAN

I can do everything through him who gives me strength.

Philippians 4:13

Play Book Assignment: Read Philippians 4:10–13

I Can Do Everything

Did you ever wonder what the favorite "favorite verse" is among Christian athletes? It's the one on this page.

Of course, there are hundreds of other verses that are cherished by believing men and women in sports, but this one is by far the number-one choice.

Why not? Sports is about strength. Sports is about doing. Sports is about getting the most out of your potential.

So when Christian athletes read a verse that says, "I can do everything through him who gives me strength," it's no mystery why they jump all over it as if it were a hanging curveball.

But what does this verse really mean?

Does it mean that a five-foot-three, 102-pound pigtailed shortstop can hit a softball over the 285-foot sign in left field?

Does it mean that a seventh-grade point guard can drive the lane and slam home a reverse dunk?

Does it mean a first-time goalkeeper can stop the other soccer team from scoring every time?

Is this verse a free pass to great athletic achievements?

Nope.

This verse really has nothing to do with sports.

What this verse is talking about is doing what pleases God. And it's telling us that Jesus is the Source for doing what pleases God. If we stay connected to Jesus, we'll have the power to do what is right.

Have you ever heard this verse: "When I am weak, then I am strong"? Sounds weird, doesn't it? To be strong, I have to be weak. But that's what Paul said in 2 Corinthians 12:10.

It's true. If we want to have God's strength (to please him, not to hit home runs), we have to admit that we're about as powerful as your grandmother batting against Randy Johnson.

Philippians 4:13 isn't like drinking Gatorade. We don't quote this verse as we're stepping to the plate, so we can pull a fastball over the left fielder's head for a double.

We quote Philippians 4:13 when we get up in the morning, so we can remind ourselves that we can't get to first base spiritually unless we rely totally on Jesus Christ.

We can't avoid temptation. We can't tell our friends about Jesus. We can't grow closer to God. We can't do good things for others. We can't do nothin' without Jesus! But we can do everything for God with Jesus.

No wonder this verse is a favorite of so many athletes.

On the Chalkboard

No Christ, no strength. Know Christ, know strength.

Speaking of Strength

Do you know who the strongest man in the world is? At one time it was a man named Paul Anderson. Paul, a strong Christian in more ways than one, could do some pretty amazing things. The strength feat that stands out as the greatest ever is this—on June 12, 1957, Paul lifted a safe full of lead off the ground with his back. The safe was placed on a table with a bunch of heavy auto parts, and he lifted the whole thing off the ground. The total weight was 6,270 pounds. That's more than the entire combined weight of the New York Yankees!

- - - - - - - - - - - - - - - - - - -*Instant Replay*

**How strong do I feel spiritually?
Do I need to get better connected to Jesus through prayer?**

Sports Stuff

Weight training has recently become popular for athletes in sports like basketball, baseball, and softball. It's been around a long time in football and other muscle sports. If you want to get involved with weight training, make sure you ask for some advice first. With basketball, you can throw off your shot if you do too much pure strength training. And with baseball and softball, you want to combine weight training with proper hitting and throwing techniques. Your coaches or your physi-

cal education teacher should be able to help you get started.
And be careful with free weights. There is the danger of getting injured if they are not used properly. If you're interested
in weight training, talk to your doctor and your gym teacher
before you start.

GAME PLAN

If anyone competes as an athlete, he does not receive the victor's crown unless he competes according to the rules.

2 Timothy 2:5

Play Book Assignment: Read Ephesians 4:25–32

Hey, Ref! Let It Go!

Have you ever played a basketball game without rules? If somebody grabs the ball and runs all the way downcourt, so what? You go up for a shot, and someone pushes you into next week. Who cares? The other team throws the ball out of bounds but just goes to get it and keeps trying to score. Big deal!

Or have you ever been to a baseball game where a play was clearly made at first base and the runner was out? Did anyone from the stands yell, "Hey, Ump! Let it go! He's a nice guy. Don't call him out!"

No sport would be any fun if everybody started to ignore the rules and just played however they wanted. And how could a game ever be played if we let the opinions of the fans control what happens in a game?

Sports have to have rules. Penalties have to be called. Fouls have to be whistled. Violations must be pointed out. Otherwise there is nothing but a jumbled mess. Did you notice that the apostle Paul knew that? He even pointed out the importance of following rules while in athletics (1 Timothy 2:5).

The same is true in our relationship with God. We get a jumbled mess there when we start to throw out God's laws and standards.

Have you ever thought that being a Christian is kind of limiting because it seems to have some rules? All you have to do is read the Ten Commandments to see that God has some pretty clear rules he wants us to use when we play the game of life. No lying. No swearing. No coveting.

Kind of like basketball. No double dribbling. No fouling. No stepping out of bounds with the ball.

The people who are in charge of the game of basketball know what they're doing. They know what's best for the game. They know it wouldn't be any fun for anyone if everybody played their own way.

God, who is in charge of our lives and knows everything about us, knows what is best for life's game. He knows how terrible things would be if everyone lived his or her own way. Ephesians 4:25–32 is a good example of some of the guidelines God has for us.

Remember that the next time you start to think it would be neat to live without any restrictions. The fun would end as soon as you discover that life without rules leads to confusion, anger, and frustration.

And nobody likes to live that way!

Trust God's guidelines for living. He knows how to make your life work.

On the Chalkboard

There's nothing worse than a life with no limits.

Speaking of Rules

One of the big differences between God's rules and human rules is that God's rules don't change. Sports rules change. Here are some rules that have been eliminated:

- At one time, you could get a runner out in baseball by throwing the ball and hitting him.
- For a while in the 1970s, it was illegal to dunk a basketball in college and high school basketball.
- Up until about fifty years ago, Major League Baseball outfielders left their gloves on the field when they went in to bat.
- In basketball's early days, there was a jump ball after every basket.

- - - - - - - - - - - - - - - - - - - -*Instant Replay*

What standards or guidelines bug me? Do I sometimes think I know better than anyone else what I should do? What's wrong with that picture?

Sports Stuff

You make the call. To be the best player you can be, you should know the rules of your sport frontward and backward. You can do this by paying close attention to games you play in or watch. Or you can buy a rule book and read it (that's pretty boring to most people). If you are old enough, you might even get a chance to umpire or referee games played by kids a lot younger than you. That will help you learn the rules fast.

> We live by faith, not by sight.
>
> 2 Corinthians 5:7

Play Book Assignment: Read 2 Corinthians 5:1—7

Blind Faith

Like a couple hundred thousand other high school students, Travis Freeman played football. Played center, in fact.

Hike the ball, pick out a defensive lineman, and keep him away from your quarterback. Same routine done by centers on teams all over his home state of Kentucky and all around the country every Friday night.

Same old same old.

Except for one thing.

Travis Freeman couldn't see.

Travis lost his sight when he was twelve years old. When he was in middle school, he asked the football coach if he could help out in some supporting position with the team.

The coach said he couldn't do that.

But he could play if he wanted. That wise coach saw potential in Travis and the spark in a young man who wasn't about to let his darkened world snuff out his dream of playing football.

Through middle school and high school, Travis continued to play. By the time he was a senior at Corbin High School, Travis had become recognized across the country for his courage. On Freeman's eighteenth birthday, the National High School Athletic Association presented Travis with the first-ever High School Athletic Hall of Fame Award—and they named it the Travis Freeman Award.

How did Travis play football? By faith.

Travis told *Sharing the Victory* magazine, " 'For we walk by faith, not by sight' (2 Corinthians 5:7) is not only a physical verse, but a spiritual one for me. Every step I take is a step on faith, that I'm not going to run into something, that there's actually going to be a floor there. The best definition of faith that I've heard is 'Faith is taking a step in the darkness and trusting that there's going to be ground there. But knowing if there's not going to be ground there, God's going to teach you how to fly.' "

Hey, if Travis can play football, why not fly?

If Travis can exercise his faith in such a huge way, what does that teach you?

What can you overcome? How hard are you willing to work to be the kind of person others notice because of your faith? And how small do some of your problems seem when compared with what Travis faced when he was twelve?

"God's got a purpose," Travis says. "God has a reason."

What's true for Travis is true for you. Trust God's reasons and work toward his purpose for you—no matter what stands in your way.

On the Chalkboard

Even in life's darkest times, you can trust the Light of the World.

Speaking of Overcoming

The world record for the 100-meter sprint by a nonsighted runner is 11.4 seconds. Graham Salmon recorded that remarkable time on September 2, 1978, in Scotland.

-------------------- -*Instant Replay*

What challenges my faith?

Sports Stuff

You'd be surprised to know how many athletes have had to overcome some kind of problem to be really good. Maybe you have something you think would keep you from succeeding. Before giving up, make sure you do everything possible to compensate for it. Talk with your parents to get their perspective on it. Give it all you have, and you may surprise yourself.

GAME PLAN

> If I had cherished sin in my heart, the Lord would not have listened.
>
> Psalm 66:18

Play Book Assignment: Read Psalm 66:16–20

Praying the Right Way

Hall of Fame baseball announcer Ernie Harwell tells this story.

The year was 1954, and Baltimore was playing the Chicago White Sox. Catching for the Orioles was Ray Murray. Behind him calling the balls and strikes was umpire Ed Hurley. With a 3–2 count on the Chicago batter, Hurley called the next pitch a ball, sending the batter to first with a walk.

Murray, who didn't like the call, turned toward Hurley, knelt down, and prayed. He said, "Dear Lord, I know that pitch was a strike. Thirty thousand people in this ballpark know it was a strike. But they have good eyes. Dear Lord, give this poor blind man a pair of good eyes, and then he'll know it was a strike."

The umpire threw Murray out of the game.

Is it possible that our prayers can be viewed by God in the same way? Does he ever ignore our prayers?

That's an unusual thought, isn't it? We're always taught that we can pray to God anytime. And we even know that he wants us to pray to him all the time.

So what's this about God not listening—just like that umpire not listening to the praying catcher?

If we have some sin that we're hanging on to and not confessing before God, he doesn't listen to our prayers.

The writer of Psalm 66 seems to be telling us that this is the deal. He talks about what happens when we "cherish" sin. That is, when we treasure a sin and keep it going when we know it's wrong.

Let's say you've been gossiping about a friend—and loving it. You talk behind his or her back, telling all kinds of nasty things about that person. And you can't wait to call your friends and exchange more dirt. That's cherishing sin.

And that will damage your prayer life with God.

So, the first prayer God needs to hear from you when you do that is: "God, forgive me for gossiping. Help me to be kind in what I say about my friend."

Then you can read the rest of Psalm 66, which says, "God has surely listened and heard my voice in prayer" (v. 19).

You'll be back to praying the right way.

On the Chalkboard

Sometimes, the next thing God wants to hear from us is "I'm sorry."

Speaking of Umpires

Sometimes umpires can be helpful. Stubby Overmire of the Detroit Tigers pitched and won the first game of a double-header. After the game, Overmire's wife arrived from out of town, and he wanted to leave to be with her. The Tiger manager told him he couldn't go. Between games, some of the players told the third-base umpire about the conflict. In the first inning of the game, the ump walked over to the dugout, looked at Overmire — who was sulking on the bench — and said, "You're out of here!" He kicked Stubby out of the game so he could be with his wife.

- - - - - - - - - - - - - - - - - - -*Instant Replay*

Do I have anything going on that is blocking my prayer life from working as it should?

Sports Stuff

The best thing to remember about umpires and referees is this short saying by former major league ump Bill Klem: "It ain't nothing until I call it." And remember this: once an official calls it, there's nothing you can do to change it, so don't look foolish trying.

If anyone says, "I love God," yet hates his brother, he is a liar.

1 John 4:20

Play Book Assignment: Read Luke 15:11–32

Brotherly Love

A long time ago, the Los Angeles Dodgers had two brothers on their team: Norm and Larry Sherry. One day during spring training, the Dodgers were playing an intrasquad game. That's when the team splits up into two groups to play a game against each other.

Norm and Larry were on opposite teams. During the scrimmage, Norm came up to bat when Larry was pitching.

One of Larry's pitches came in high and tight, and Norm went crashing to the ground to get out of the way. As he got up and dusted himself off, he turned to his brother and shouted, "Do that again, and I'll call Mom."

Sound familiar?

Obviously, these two major-league players were joking around, but you can imagine that when they were growing up, they had their share of sibling squabbles. And many of them probably ended up just like that one.

If you have a brother or sister, you know exactly what this is all about.

"Mom! Michael's in my room!"

"Well, Meredith hit me, and I'm just going after her!"

To which Mom replies, "Michael, don't hit your sister. And Meredith, stay out of his room. You know the rules."

Of course at that time, she'll get the meek reply from both siblings.

"Oh, okay, Mom. We're sorry."

Right. And it's going to rain hundred-dollar bills tomorrow!

It's probably more like: "That's not fair! She hit me, and I get to belt her one."

Followed by, "MOM! Michael just took one of my CDs."

You get the picture. No, you probably *live* the picture.

What is the deal with all the fighting between siblings? Is it because they want their parents to have a heart attack? Are they looking for ways to be grounded? Is it written on their contract that brothers and sisters have to go at it?

Did you ever think about the prodigal son story as a lesson about sibling rivalry? Well, think about it. The younger brother gets his money ahead of time and goes out and blows it. He does what little brothers often do. He makes an immature choice. (Okay, if you're an older sibling, stop gloating.) Then, when young bro comes home, Dad throws a massive party. Guess what big bro does? He gets really jealous.

In both cases, the brothers were each looking out only for themselves. It takes a wise father to help the boys see what's really happening.

Dad tells his firstborn, "Look, I love you too, but you're always here. You've always enjoyed all the great things we have. Your little sib was dead, and now he is alive (Luke 11:32). Let's party!" In other words, let's get along. You are both well taken care of.

There's a verse in 1 Thessalonians 5 that should be the motto of every brother and sister. It says, "Live in peace with each other" (v. 13). A little brotherly and sisterly love goes a long way at home.

On the Chalkboard

If you have the peace of God in your heart, try letting peace rule your life at home.

Speaking of Brothers

Lots of sibling combinations have played professional sports. For example, did you know that Mark McGwire has a brother, Dan, who used to be an NFL quarterback? Or that the NBA's Reggie Miller has a sister, Cheryl, who played for the US Olympic basketball team (1984) and coaches in the WNBA? And did you know that they have a brother who played for the California Angels in the late 1980s? Did you know that the NFL's Cris Carter has a brother, Butch, who coaches the Toronto Raptors?

- - - - - - - - - - - - - - - - - - -*Instant Replay*

Do I enjoy irritating my siblings? What can help me realize that this isn't right?

Sports Stuff

Sometimes the best thing a younger sibling has is the example of an older brother or sister. If you have an older brother or sister who is an athlete, watch and learn from him or her. Ask questions about how to get better in your sport. And what may help even more, practice against your brother or sister. You'll be surprised how much you'll learn from an older sibling. But you have to live at peace with each other first.

> But those who suffer [God] delivers in their suffering; he speaks to them in their affliction.
>
> Job 36:15

Play Book Assignment: Read Psalm 66:8–12

Playing with Pain

While cruising the grocery store aisles the other day, I saw somebody I know.

No, it wasn't my next-door neighbor or somebody I work with.

It was Michelle Akers, famous soccer player with the US National team. An acquaintance through the contact I've had with her as managing editor of *Sports Spectrum* magazine, Michelle stands out as one of the sports world's nicest people.

There she was in the grocery store, up on the shelf.

She was gracing the cover of a box of Wheaties.

Whenever I think of Michelle, I think of three words: "playing with pain." She is one athlete who stands out above all others as determined to compete despite the discomfort she is going through.

Michelle has had numerous knee surgeries. She's had more concussions than quarterback Steve Young. She's had shoulder separations and black eyes and who knows how many other disastrous things happen to her body. And above all that, she suffers from chronic fatigue and immune dysfunction syndrome (CFIDS). That means she is always dog tired and has to pace herself just to live a normal life, let alone play world-class soccer.

In discussing her ability to continue despite the pain, she quotes a famous French impressionist painter Renoir, who said, "The pain passes, but the beauty remains."

Renoir also knew about pain. He had arthritis so bad that at one point he had to have his paintbrushes tied to his fingers because it hurt too much to hold them. Yet he became one of the best-known artists in the world.

Do you have some kind of pain that hampers you? Listen to what Michelle says: "Pain grabs our full and immediate attention. It also brings us to the end of ourselves. When this happens, we either become closed and bitter or we become more open to God's promises."

What hurts in your life? Can you trust God to help you make it through? And can you allow that pain to make you a better person, as it has done with Michelle? Are you willing to let God bring you "to a place of abundance" as the psalmist said in Psalm 66:12?

"God will never shield us from life's adversities, because pain can produce the beauty of true character and a deeper, more powerful faith," Michelle says. That kind of attitude can make us want to go ahead and play despite the pain.

On the Chalkboard

What God can teach us through trouble is worth the pain.

More about Michelle

Here are some of the honors that have come Michelle's way:

- 1985 ESPN Athlete of the Year
- 1987 MVP, NCAA Final Four
- 1988 Hermann Trophy, college soccer's best player
- 1991 US Soccer Federation Female Athlete of the Year
- 1991 FIFA World Cup Golden Boot award
- 1998 CONCACAF Top Woman Soccer Player of the twentieth century

- -*Instant Replay*

What pain or trouble would I rather just get rid of? Can I see that God is teaching me anything through it?

Sports Stuff

As an athlete, you need to learn the difference between something that hurts and something that is damaged. Sometimes, when you have a sore muscle or a slight sprain, you can play through the pain. Other times, when some part of your body hurts, it's because there is damage that you can make worse by continuing to compete. Talk to your parents or coach about your pain. They can help you determine whether to keep going or to get some medical attention.

GAME PLAN

Be diligent in these matters; give yourself wholly to them, so that everyone may see your progress.

1 Timothy 4:15

Play Book Assignment: Read 1 Timothy 4:11–16

Stretching It

Whenever my family goes jogging, there's usually a little ritual that takes place before we hit the road. I walk out to the end of the driveway and wait for everybody else to join me so we can get started. But they're all pushing against the house or the basketball pole, stretching out their legs.

They always tell me, "Dad, you have to stretch before you run."

I always say, "I've never stretched in my life. I'm not going to start now." And it's true, through high school and college, playing baseball and basketball, I never stretched. I just ran out on the court and started firing away.

But I'm not proud of it. I'm wrong. Fortunate, but wrong.

Most physical trainers will tell you that it's important to warm up and stretch, and then when you're done, warm down. If you don't, funny things can happen to your muscles. Although I never pulled a hamstring or any other muscle (my kids would say it's because I don't have any), I wasn't training properly.

Stretching is not only good for athletes, but it's also good for Christians. You and I need to stretch our spiritual muscles. We need to find things that will challenge us and make us depend on God more and more.

How can you stretch your spiritual muscles?

It's a matter of devotion (1 Timothy 4:13) and diligence (v. 15).

One way to stretch those spiritual muscles would be to decide that you're going to tell an unsaved friend about Jesus. That will stretch you! It's easy to talk to your friend about the other kids at school, about the latest movie, or about some sports star you both like. But it's a major streeeeeeeetch to say, "Do you know Jesus Christ?"

Another way to stretch your spiritual muscles is by making plans to learn something new about the Bible or about faith in general. Let's say, for instance, that you want to know what the Bible says about jealousy. So you take a notebook, grab a Bible with a concordance, and do a little digging. It's not easy, but it's worthwhile. And it will stretch you!

You can get by without stretching. You can be a Christian who is just doing the basics and getting by. But if you stretch your spiritual muscles, you'll please God, you'll be proud of yourself, and you'll find your faith more exciting.

So don't do like I do when I go jogging. Take the time to stretch. It'll feel sooooo good.

On the Chalkboard

Expand your spiritual horizons, or you'll find your world growing smaller, not bigger.

Speaking of Exercise

One of the greatest generals in US history was Douglas MacArthur. He served in World War II and helped return the Philippine Islands to the control of the United States. Each day, he followed this routine: Every morning he began with a round of calisthenics. He also walked several miles each day. In his mind, regular exercise was essential for making a person well rounded.

- - - - - - - - - - - - - - - - - - -*Instant Replay*

What can I do that will help me stretch my spiritual muscles?

Sports Stuff

According to Dr. Kenneth Cooper, one of the foremost authorities on exercise and good training, here are the basics of stretching:

1. Movements should be done slowly, without bouncing or fast motion.
2. Try to achieve a full range of motion.
3. Work up gradually to your full stretching ability.
4. Hold your maximum stretch for fifteen seconds, and then slowly relax.

I gave you milk, not solid food, for you were not yet ready for it.

1 Corinthians 3:2

Play Book Assignment: Read 1 Corinthians 3:1–2

What's Eating You?

The answer to the question in today's title might be, "What you're eating."

Huh?

"What's Eating You?" is "What you're eating"? What does that mean?

It means that sometimes what we put into our bodies doesn't do us much good. Instead, it harms us.

Nothing wrong with a nice big Oreo once in a while, but if that's all you were to eat, you're body would be a mess. It wouldn't like a full diet of such poor nutrition. In that case, what you were eating would "eat up" your body.

How good are you at knowing what is good for you?

Do you think you might do better than a bunch of NBA players? A few years ago, some NBA stars were asked to take a nutrition test. Here are some of the questions:

a. What fluid is best after a game?

b. How much fluid do you need daily?

c. Which fluid is best during a game?

d. How much fluid is best one hour before a game?

e. After a late game, what food is best among a hamburger, pizza, or Mexican?

f. Before a game, what food is best?

g. What is the best pizza?

h. What dessert is best among a chocolate cake, homemade cookies, or a banana split?

The athletes got fewer than half the questions right. They didn't know what food and drink was best for their bodies.

Likewise, sometimes we as Christians don't know what's best for helping us grow spiritually. We could ask some questions:

• How much time should I read the Bible each day?

• What kind of music helps me think about God?

• What kind of entertainment choices turn me away from God?

• What are the best kinds of things to read if I want to get stronger in my relationship with God?

Did you read what Paul said in 1 Corinthians 3:2? He told the people that they were still eating baby food when they should have been eating steak. (Well, okay, he didn't mention Gerber and filet mignon, but that's the point of what he was saying.)

It's easy to develop an appetite for food that isn't the best and to be happy with taking a spiritual bottle instead of chomping on meat. But then that makes us spiritual weaklings who can't even make a spiritual layup.

Like those NBA players learned by taking that test, we should learn to eat right spiritually. Then what we're eating will help us grow up the right way.

On the Chalkboard

Why be on a starvation diet when God has a whole banquet of blessings waiting for us?

The Answers to the NBA Test

a. orange juice, sports drinks, water

b. four quarts

c. water, sports drinks

d. two cups

e. pizza

f. chicken and spaghetti; four to six hours before the game

g. cheese

h. banana split; at least it has potassium

- -*Instant Replay*

Am I spiritually hungry? Am I eating the right things?

Sports Stuff

Eating right before a sports competition is essential, because that meal (and even the one before) will give you the energy you need. One aspect of this is proper hydration, or taking in fluids. Having proper fluids in your body helps you not get tired as fast—that's why you need to drink two cups of liquid an hour before the competition. The meal you want to eat a few hours before competition is one with a solid high-carbohydrate level.

GAME PLAN

We can comfort those in any trouble with the comfort we ourselves have received from God.

2 Corinthians 1:4

Play Book Assignment: Read 2 Corinthians 1:3—7

What about Bob?

More than likely, you know someone named Bob. It's a common name, so you probably have an Uncle Bob or a cousin named Bob or a friend of the family named Bob or a next-door neighbor named Bob.

But there is one Bob you need to know about, because he's a special person. He's the kind of person who can teach you a lot about how to handle tough times.

Bob Bardwell was twenty-six years old when a construction accident left him paralyzed from the waist down. He had been a successful college wrestler, even getting a chance to try out for the US Olympic team.

The accident that cost him the use of his legs, though, didn't stop him from continuing as an athlete. Bob became an accomplished wheelchair marathon racer. He raced in the Boston Marathon, and he won the Chicago Marathon. All told, he finished more than one hundred marathons.

Besides that, Bardwell has done more things than most people could do in two lifetimes. He started and runs a youth camp, he is a popular motivational speaker, and he is the father of four girls—including triplets.

But the best thing about Bob is his faith and his attitude. He sees what happened to him as a way to help people—especially kids. "Instead of being five feet nine inches, I'm four feet tall," he says, referring to his height in a wheelchair. "How tall are kids? Just my height! We talk eye-to-eye, and I can easily put my arm around them, which makes for real special times. I know I've been able to reach the lives of many youth and adults as a result of my injury."

Here's what one young man, Noel, wrote to Bob: "Whenever my situation gets to me, you come to mind. Many times in the privacy of your mind, you must long to be free of your disability. Thank you for allowing the Lord to use your disability to make some of my 'struggling moments' easier."

What about Bob? Bob is an example of how God wants us to live. Trusting that whatever happens to us can be used somehow to honor him.

What struggle are you facing today? Could God be getting you ready to encourage someone else by the way you deal with your trouble?

That's the plan, according to 2 Corinthians 1. Doing that will help you make the best of any bad situation.

On the Chalkboard

Our troubles are worthwhile if they lead us to help others.

Speaking of Marathons

When a wheelchair racer goes out onto the course for a marathon, he or she faces struggles non-wheelchair competitors don't. One is that they need to know a little about repairing their chair. If it gets a flat or has some other problem, the racer has to figure out how to fix it and get back in the race. Another is that they have to have very, very strong arms. In the course of racing 26.2 miles, a wheelchair marathoner will generate more than four thousand arm strokes as he or she keeps the wheels rolling. Try that sometime!

- - - - - - - - - - - - - - - - - - - -*Instant Replay*

What difficulty do I sometimes wish I didn't have? How can I use that to encourage someone else?

Sports Stuff

Whether running or wheeling in a marathon, training is the key. If you want to be a long-distance racer of either kind, you need to accumulate a lot of miles. In Bob Bardwell's first three years of wheelchair racing, he averaged seventy-five miles a week of training. For a runner, it's important as well to have a goal of twenty- to twenty-five miles a week or so, depending on your event. Make sure you get the advice of a good coach who understands how much you should run at your age.

Show proper respect to everyone.

1 Peter 2:17

Play Book Assignment: Read 1 Samuel 24:1–7

Being a Fan

Are you a sports fan? Do you like to go to the game and watch your favorite team in action?

Jim Tunney, a longtime NFL referee, would like a word with you. After years of being down on the field listening to what people say to the men and women in stripes, he came up with this description of a fan:

"My definition of a fan is the kind of guy who will scream at you from the sixtieth row of the bleachers because he thinks you missed a marginal holding call in the center of the interior line, and then after the game he won't be able to find his car in the parking lot."

Sports fans can be irritating people. They think they know the rules better than the people who were hired to enforce them.

Let's say you're watching a basketball game. A player dribbles the ball up court. When she gets to the half-court line, she steps into the frontcourt with one foot. Then she pulls it back into the backcourt. The referee just watches. No whistle. No nothing.

Well, about half of the fans rooting for the team on defense just about come unglued. They stand up, wave their hands back and forth, and scream, "Over and back! That's over and back!" And they are all over the ref like a bad case of measles.

But you know what? The ref is right. You have to have the ball and both feet over the line before you're considered to be in the frontcourt.

Yet the ref is made to look like a doofus.

Is that right to do to someone?

What is our responsibility before God when it comes to referees? As you grow up and become a more intense sports fan, you might need to consider this question. Right now, going to a game is mostly a social deal; you're there because your friends are. And maybe you can't figure out why all those adults seem to be so upset about what the refs are doing.

Yet even now, it's important to develop the right attitude toward the people in authority — even at a ball game.

The Old Testament character David showed us an important lesson about getting along with those you don't agree with. He was being pursued by King Saul, who liked David about as much as the New York Knicks like the Miami Heat.

David and his men were in the back of a cave when Saul's men entered the cave. While Saul was distracted, David cut off a piece of his robe. Soon after, though, David felt bad about it, saying, "The LORD forbid that I should do such a thing to my master" (1 Samuel 24:6). David decided that agreeing with the person in charge wasn't necessary for respecting him.

As a fan, each of us should show proper respect to everyone—especially to those in authority. So show restraint. It's another way to demonstrate the difference God is making in your life.

On the Chalkboard

When a fan gives a referee a piece of his mind, it's usually a piece he can't afford to lose.

Speaking of Officials

Here's how an old-time baseball umpire summed up what he believed people thought of him. "What a life. You can't call it a dog's life because most people like dogs. Even a criminal on trial is considered innocent until they convict him. But look at us. Lower than the scum of the earth, worthy of no man's praise and every man's scorn."

-Instant Replay

What kind of fan am I? Do I show proper respect for referees when I'm watching? When I'm playing?

Sports Stuff

Fans should never approach a referee or official, but sometimes, a player or coach can do so. If that happens, though, it must be done with respect and dignity. A player, especially the team captain, should be able to approach an official during a time-out and calmly mention something that may be important. "Sir, their center is pushing our center every time he gets the ball. I know it's hard to see everything, but could you look for that?" This kind of comment from a captain or a coach is usually met with respect by an official. The key is never to show up a referee and put him or her in a position where the ref is made to look bad because of your actions.

Greater love has no one than this, that he lay down his life for his friends.

John 15:13

Play Book Assignment: Read Acts 6:8–14; 7:51–60

To Die For

You've probably heard the phrase "It's to die for." Usually when someone is using these words, that person is referring to an outlandishly delicious dessert or some piece of clothing that was spotted at the mall.

Or it could even be a person.

Rinngg! "Hello." "Hi, Lauren, this is Erica. I saw Corey today at the pool. Whew! He's to die for."

It's a nice little line, and it expresses a feeling of admiration or respect or appreciation for something really nice.

But it takes on an entirely different meaning when it is said seriously by someone who has thought about whether something is truly important enough to die for.

Listen, for instance, to one of basketball's all-time best players, David Robinson, as he talks about his love for his Savior, Jesus Christ.

"I'm very convicted, very committed to what I believe. I would die for what I believe. I know about Jesus Christ. I know about the motivation for my life. If I'm not willing to give up my life for the Lord, then there's nothing else in my life worth standing for."

Wow! To Mr. Robinson, faith in Jesus Christ is worth dying for.

That's not something you hear much about these days, is it?

But you probably know about one person in the book of Acts who gave up his life for Jesus Christ. His name was Stephen, and he stood his ground against the people who were accusing him of doing wrong. In fact, he preached to them about Jesus — more than they wanted to know. So much more that they grew angry enough to kill him.

Although we don't hear much about this kind of thing happening today, it does. There are countries in other parts of the world where Christians are being murdered for their faith right now. Some people have concluded that more Christians were martyred in the twentieth century than in the previous nineteen centuries.

So, even though the twenty-first century seems like a modern time, people still face something as old and as awful as being a martyr.

You may not ever be called on to defend your faith before a group of people who will kill you if you say the wrong thing, and David Robinson might not ever have to do that either.

But it's important to have that kind of conviction. And most of all, it's vital that you know who is really "to die for." Jesus.

On the Chalkboard

Jesus died for us. The least we can do is live for him.

More on the Admiral

David Robinson isn't afraid to speak out about his faith in Christ. Here's what he says about that: "The Lord calls different people to do different things. I just happen to have a big mouth, so I like to talk about my faith. I don't like to have secrets. If something is great, I feel I can share it with people. I really have a burden to see people's eyes opened, to see them grow in the Lord."

- - - - - - - - - - - - - - - - - - - -*Instant Replay*

Have I ever thought of what I would do if I were asked to stand up for Jesus if my life were on the line? What would I do?

Sports Stuff

There are lots of different ways to get in shape for your sport. Running, biking, swimming. But David Robinson has a rather unorthodox way of keeping in shape during the off-season. He hikes. He likes to climb hills and explore. So, maybe that will give you another way to get those muscles toned up.

GAME PLAN

> What benefit did you reap at that time from the things you are now ashamed of? Those things result in death.
>
> Romans 6:21

Play Book Assignment: Read Romans 6:19–23

What Happened to Bernie

You've probably never heard of Bernie Carbo.

That's because you're too young to know about the dramatic home run he hit in the sixth game of the 1975 World Series.

The 1975 series, some people say, was the most exciting one ever. But even if it wasn't, it had tons of drama.

Like what Bernie did, for instance.

The Cincinnati Reds had a 3–2 lead over the Boston Red Sox in the series, and a 6–3 lead in game six as the Red Sox came to bat in the bottom of the eighth inning. They put two runners on base for Carbo, who had started his baseball career with

Cincinnati and had already hit one home run in the series. All Bernie did was to step up and pound a game-tying three-run blast into the left center-field seats. The Red Sox won the game 7−6 in the twelfth inning when catcher Carlton Fisk hit a home run that hit the foul pole.

The Reds won the next game and the World Championship, but that sixth game has never been forgotten by true baseball fans.

For a long time, Bernie Carbo was forgotten. He stuck around the major leagues until 1980, but then he was gone. Washed up at the age of thirty-three. Struggling with a serious addiction to drugs, suffering the death of both parents, and mourning the breakup of his marriage, Carbo was mired in trouble.

In 1992, he decided that life wasn't worth living. The drugs had drained him of any self-respect or desire. Yet two of his former friends recognized his situation and got him into a treatment program.

It was there that Bernie finally met someone who could help him. A retired preacher told him about Jesus Christ. And a nurse helped him pray to trust Jesus. With a new look at life, Bernie started his own baseball ministry and set off to live for Jesus.

Drugs robbed Bernie of several good years. Jesus gave him hope. What a difference!

Don't ever let anyone tell you that drugs won't hurt you. And don't let a day go by without thanking Jesus for being your Lord and Savior.

What happened to Bernie finally turned out for good because he finally met the source of all that is right: Jesus.

"I love Jesus because he gave me new life," says Bernie. We can do the same.

On the Chalkboard

Jesus can protect us from anything our world wants to throw at us.

More about Bernie

After trusting Jesus, Bernie started the Diamond Club, which he wanted to use to "tell the greatest story ever told through the greatest game ever played." During his career, Carbo hit ninety-six home runs. He hit twenty-one home runs in his first year with the Reds.

- -*Instant Replay*

Am I ever tempted to try substances that I know are not good for me? When I am tempted, how can I let my relationship with Christ protect me?

Sports Stuff

Bernie Carbo got started on drugs by taking pills that were made available to him in the clubhouse of major-league teams. To keep your body clean and pure, don't experiment with any drugs anyone offers you. Take only the medications your doctor prescribes. Anything someone else offers as a way of enhancing your performance, relaxing you, or making you feel better is dangerous. The pills Carbo started with were performance-enhancing drugs, and he went to worse things from there.

For if the willingness is there, the gift is acceptable according to what one has, not according to what he does not have.

2 Corinthians 8:12

Play Book Assignment: Read Luke 21:1–4

Why Give?

How much allowance do you get in a week?

Oops. Did I hear someone say, "None"?

Sorry to open up such a sore spot with you. But, hey, you do have some money, isn't that true? You get money for mowing the grass or washing the car or helping Mom with the wash or something!

Or perhaps you have a paper route. Or you shovel sidewalks. Somehow, you earn money.

Who knows, maybe you have your own website called E-kid, and you've figured out a way to get people to send you money.

The point is, you have some money.

What are you doing with it?

Former Major League Baseball player Sid Bream was walking along a crowded area of San Diego one day when he met a couple of young boys who were looking for a handout. (Hey, there's another idea!)

Anyway, when Bream stopped to ask the boys why they weren't at home but were out on the street begging, one of them showed him his arms, which had slash marks on them. The boy explained that his dad beat him.

Bream didn't hesitate to pull some money from his pocket and give it to the boys. They had a real need for his help.

Here's how Bream described the help he provided. "I was helping them to show them how much God loved them and how much he loved us."

But there's more to Bream's giving ways. He also said, "Money, power, and big houses aren't going to mean much when our lives are over and we're standing before Christ."

Have you ever sat down and thought through what God expects of you when it comes to giving? Have you begun to develop a habit of taking some of your money and giving part of it to help God's work?

When you think about the comparison between how much a major leaguer can give and how much you can give, you might think your little bit of money won't do any good.

But that's not the point. The point is that God expects each of us to give out of love for him and concern for his work.

Think about that poor widow Jesus watched as she deposited her two coins in the offering box. She must have known her little gift couldn't feed the poor or help much with the temple treasury. But she gave. And Jesus said, "I tell you the truth, . . . this poor widow has put in more than all the others."

Why give? We do it not to show off or to make a spectacle but to show our love for God and our concern for others.

You can do that with allowance money, paper-route money, or the money you collect from turning in empty pop cans. It's not the amount but the heart behind it that counts.

On the Chalkboard

When you give sincerely and in love, you can't give too much — or too little.

Speaking of Sid Bream

On October 14, 1992, Sid Bream scored the biggest run of his life. His Atlanta Braves were playing the Pittsburgh Pirates. It was the seventh game of the National League Championship Series. The winner would go to the World Series. The loser would go away, never to be heard from again. Going into the bottom of the ninth inning, Pittsburgh was ahead 2–0. The Braves loaded the bases. They got one run through a sacrifice fly. Then, with two outs, Francisco Cabrera slapped a hit into the outfield. The runner on third scored with the tying run, but then came Sid Bream lumbering around third. He had bad knees, so this wasn't easy. Yet on he chugged. The throw came toward the plate, Sid slid. Safe! The Atlanta Braves won the National League pennant.

- - - - - - - - - - - - - - - - - - -*Instant Replay*

Have I started making a habit of giving to God's work from all of my resources, including my money?

Sports Stuff

As an athlete and a follower of Jesus Christ, you might some-times wonder if you can do both successfully. But one thing you have to do is decide what kind of athlete you're going to be. Sid Bream says that Christian athletes should be champions. "I don't think that because we're Christians, we should be slack in our competitiveness. I think God wants us to be the very best. I want to show people that Christians are champions."

GAME PLAN

For I am not seeking my own good but the good of many.

1 Corinthians 10:33

Play Book Assignment: Read 1 Corinthians 10:23–26, 31–33

Sticking to Your Guns

Please take this quiz before you begin today's reading.
Rugby is:

a. A game played on Persian rugs
b. A toy that was made popular by *The Rugrats Movie*
c. A game that looks like football without the helmets
d. A small animal that grows in Australia

Since you're reading a sports devotional book, it can be assumed that you're pretty smart about sports. And if you are, you know that the answer is "c."

Rugby is a fascinating sport played in many countries of the world. It's a rough-and-tumble sport in which the athletes run into each other, tackle each other, and in many ways mix it up with each other as they try to advance an oblong ball down the field. It's kind of like American football without the helmets and pads—and without huddles.

One of the best rugby players in the world is Michael Jones, who played for a team called the New Zealand All Blacks, a team named for their dark uniforms. One year, Jones and his team were in England to play in the World Cup. This is the worldwide tournament of rugby, similar to the competition of the same name in soccer.

The All Blacks advanced to the semifinals of the World Cup, and they were scheduled to play on a Sunday. It would possibly be the biggest game of Jones's life, but that didn't matter. He felt that he shouldn't play on Sunday. He felt that Sunday is the Lord's Day, and it should be honored by going to church, not playing rugby.

Rugby is a big sport in New Zealand, so the folks from the homeland weren't at all happy to have their star flanker out of the game. But Jones stuck to his decision. He felt the attention he was receiving was "a marvelous means of telling everyone what the Lord means to me."

He didn't play.

Standing up for what you believe isn't easy. People say mean things. They criticize. They mock. They try to make you feel silly.

Don't let them. If you know what you're doing is right, stick to your guns. The Bible writer James said, "Anyone, then, who knows the good he ought to do and doesn't do it, sins" (James 4:17). If you have a conviction that God has clearly showed you what to do, he will honor you if you do it.

Stick to your guns.

On the Chalkboard

Being right isn't something decided on by a vote of your friends.

More about Rugby

Actually, there are two games of rugby that are played around the world. One is the Rugby Football Union and the other is the National Rugby League. The major difference between the two leagues for many years was that in the Rugby Union all the players had to be amateurs, which means they couldn't be paid. Not long ago, that rule was changed, and salaries were allowed. Most of the rules for both brands of rugby are the same or similar.

- - - - - - - - - - - - - - - - - - -*Instant Replay*

**What have I failed to stand up for recently?
What have I stood up for recently?**

Sports Stuff

What new sport have you tried recently? Perhaps you're a soccer player, but you've never tried golf or tennis. Of course, there is always rugby or lacrosse or water polo. Athletes who are good in one sport often find that they can play several. Why not give a new one a try?

GAME PLAN

God chose the foolish things of the world to shame the wise.

1 Corinthians 1:27

Play Book Assignment: Read 1 Corinthians 1:26–31

Felipe's Fish

What would you think of a person who says the biggest achievement of his life was catching a fish?

You'd probably put this person in the "get a life" category and wonder why he didn't do something else with the other days and years God gave him.

But then what if you were told that this person—whose big moment was pulling a scaly finned creature out of the water—also had achieved the following things:

- Played seventeen years of Major League Baseball
- Banged out 2,101 hits
- Had a career batting average of .286

- Won more than four hundred games as a big-league manager
- Was the National League Manager of the Year

Young Felipe followed his dad, Jose, out into the waters of the Caribbean Sea. Jose absolutely had to catch some fish because his family had no other food. A storm was coming, and the opportunity for fishing was growing short. Time after time, Jose threw his line into the water, only to come up with nothing. At his side, Felipe begged and begged his papa for one try. Finally, Jose gave his son a chance.

Felipe tossed his line into the water. As soon as it hit, he felt that unmistakable tug on the other end. He hauled in the line and discovered that a five-pound grouper was attached to the hook. The family would have plenty to eat.

Little Felipe grew up to be Felipe Alou, the player and manager described earlier. Yet that fishing expedition with his father remained important to him because it has always reminded him to remain humble—and that every provision is from God.

In the 1990s, Alou was the manager of the Montreal Expos. One year, 1994, the Expos had the best record in baseball when the players decided to go on strike. Alou's best chance to make it to the World Series was gone. The team needed money, so they got rid of many of Alou's best players.

For a man who was at one time one fish from starvation, this wasn't a life-and-death problem. He said simply, "The Lord seemed to say to me, 'I didn't send you here to win the pennant; I sent you here to be a witness for me.'"

And that's what he has been. Felipe's fish taught him what is important in life. His baseball team taught him what God wanted him to be. Simple lessons. Simple truths.

> ## On the Chalkboard
> It's not the big things in life that show what kind of
> people we are, but the little things.

More About Felipe

Felipe wasn't the only one of Jose Alou's kids who played in
the major leagues. Brothers Matty and Jesus ("Hey-soos") also
played in the majors. At one time, they were all members of
the San Francisco Giants. Felipe's son, Moises, is a star who has
played for Montreal and Houston. His uncle, Mel Rojas, even
played in the majors.

- - - - - - - - - - - - - - - - - - - -Instant Replay

What do I consider my biggest accomplishment so far?

Sports Stuff

Felipe's brother Matty was considered one of the best hitters of
his day. He was a slap hitter, meaning he hit the ball all over
the field. That worked best for him because he was small (five
foot nine and 160 pounds). That's a good technique to learn if
you want to hit for a better batting average. To do that, you try
to hit the ball where it's pitched. If it's outside, punch it to the
opposite field, for instance. This kind of hitter usually knows
how to bunt well too.

Therefore, as God's chosen people, holy and dearly loved, clothe yourselves with compassion, kindness, humility, gentleness and patience.

Colossians 3:12

Play Book Assignment: Read Acts 11:27–30

Help for Mrs. McFarland

A few years ago, Heath Shuler was expected to be an up-and-coming star in the NFL. He was drafted by the Washington Redskins, and they paid him a whole bunch of money.

Problem was, things didn't work out for Heath and football. He didn't play too well in Washington, and then he gave it a try in New Orleans and then Oakland. Finally, he gave up and went home to Tennessee.

But just because he didn't become the big star everyone thought he would doesn't mean he's not a good guy.

Just ask Bessie McFarland.

Mrs. McFarland, a great-grandmother, was trying to get from Baltimore to Knoxville, Tennessee, but her flight was canceled. Shuler, who was still playing for the Redskins at the time and was also trying to get to Knoxville, overheard Mrs. McFarland talking to a ticket agent about her trouble.

He asked Mrs. McFarland if she wanted to stick with him, because he was going to try to figure out a way to get to Knoxville. So with Mrs. McFarland by his side, Heath got two tickets to Atlanta. When he got there, he talked the airline people into holding the last plane to Knoxville so they could catch it.

When they got to Knoxville, Heath called a cab for Mrs. McFarland and made sure she got home safely.

A believer in Jesus Christ since he was seven years old, Shuler surprised no one with his kindness and generosity.

What he did clearly show us is the importance of caring for those who need our help.

Sometimes the help we need to give is money, as the Christians did in Acts 11 for people living in a land where there was a famine. Sometimes we can help others by giving of our abilities, like you might do if you and your friends from church go to a nursing home to sing for the people there. Sometimes we can provide a little elbow grease, like you can do by knocking on a neighbor's door and asking if you can rake her leaves.

Compassion, kindness, humility, gentleness, and patience. These are all things we can give others—from Mrs. McFarland to your neighbor to your friends at school. Follow the example of Heath Shuler. Help someone make it through the day.

On the Chalkboard

The biggest blessing received when you give is the joy you will experience.

Speaking of Quarterbacks

Over the past decade and more, there have been several Christian quarterbacks in the NFL. Among them have been Randall Cunningham, Minnesota Vikings; Jon Kitna, Seattle Seahawks; Kurt Warner, St. Louis Rams; Mark Brunell, Jacksonville Jaguars; Trent Dilfer, Tampa Bay Buccaneers; Kent Graham, New York Giants; Danny Wuerffel, New Orleans Saints; Jim Harbaugh, San Diego Chargers; Steve Stenstrom, San Francisco 49ers.

-------------------- -*Instant Replay*

What have I done recently for someone who didn't ask for my help? What can I do today?

Sports Stuff

Do you think you'd be a good quarterback? (Girls can answer these questions too.) Here are seven qualities you would have to have:

1. Strong hands and good arm strength
2. Accuracy in throwing
3. The mental capacity to understand complex plays

4. The ability to look over a defense, figure out what it's doing, and respond
5. Toughness
6. Leadership qualities
7. A hard head